R. B Smith

Hugging to Music

A Story from Life

R. B Smith

Hugging to Music
A Story from Life

ISBN/EAN: 9783337084615

Printed in Europe, USA, Canada, Australia, Japan

Cover: Foto ©ninafisch / pixelio.de

More available books at **www.hansebooks.com**

"An ef thar wa'nt the parson learnin' Hank the Lord's Prayer, an' my Hank, a infer del, goin' it fur all he wuz wo'th. Somehow I yanked off my hat jess ez if I wuz in a meetin' heouse, I wuz so mad!" (Page 19.)

HUGGING TO MUSIC.

A STORY FROM LIFE.

BY

AN AMERICAN OBSERVER.

ILLUSTRATED BY THE AUTHOR.

UNIVERSITY PUBLISHING COMPANY,
FRANKLIN SQUARE,
NEW YORK.
1890.

ENTERED ACCORDING TO ACT OF CONGRESS, BY THE AUTHOR, JUNE, 1889,
IN THE OFFICE OF THE LIBRARIAN OF CONGRESS AT WASHINGTON.

All Rights Reserved.

FULLY PROTECTED BY COPYRIGHT IN GREAT BRITAIN AND ALL BRITISH
PROVINCES. ALSO IN EIGHT OTHER PRINCIPAL GOVERNMENTS.

Translations and All Rights Reserved.

INTRODUCTION.

The characters in my story are evolved from life. Joe Jungle and little Hank are studies made in a mining district of California. As with the sketches of others, I trust the public will find interest, and if, amidst pernicious winds of modern thought, a stray seed of the "Wayback's" experience should fall on fertile soil, where hope in that home beyond has been cruelly blasted, let us trust it may spring forth into sweet blossoms, which shall waft back perfumes of regenerating faith in a Divine Creator.

THE AUTHOR.

CONTENTS.

CHAPTER I.
JOE JUNGLE, THE WAYBACK INFIDEL, . . 9

CHAPTER II.
ONE VICTIM, ... 24

CHAPTER III.
DISCUSSING THE WALTZ, ... 36

CHAPTER IV.
THE BALL, ... 51

CHAPTER V.
THE LAST WALTZ, ... 64

CHAPTER VI.
THE HUSBAND'S RETURN, ... 71

CHAPTER VII.
A THIRD VICTIM, ... 75

CHAPTER VIII.
FIRE AT SEA, ... 90

CHAPTER IX.
SAVED, ... 100

CHAPTER X.
No News, ... 107

CHAPTER XI.
The Burial at Sea, ... 125

CHAPTER XII.
The Prodigal, ... 138

CHAPTER XIII.
London, ... 149

CHAPTER XIV.
The New Joe Jungle, ... 159

CHAPTER XV.
Joe Jungle Adopts a Daughter, . 173

CHAPTER XVI.
The Rector, ... 196

CHAPTER XVII.
The Tragic Meeting, . . . 202

CHAPTER XVIII.
Unforgiving, ... 211

CHAPTER XIX.
Ruby's Instinct, ... 233

PROLOGUE.

Victoria Lennox entered the conservatory on the arm of Deluth, as the latter exclaimed:

"Deny it! deny it if you can!"

The dreamy, waltz-intoxicated Victoria was speechless.

A grasp on the portière at her side relaxed, and Jack Lennox fell senseless at the feet of his terrified wife.

HUGGING TO MUSIC.

CHAPTER I.

JOE JUNGLE, THE WAYBACK INFIDEL.

AN eastbound train was whizzing over the Rocky Mountains at such velocity it seemed miraculous it should not be swept from the dizzy pinnacles to death-yawning arms below. Gentlemen tourists were gazing upward at the Devil's Slide, and commenting on Satan's tobogganing shoot, when they retired to the smoking-room to play cards. There they encountered an ally in the queerest specimen of a "Wayback American," as he took pride in terming himself, whose favorite game was draw poker.

He was such an example of the early West, all were alert, lest he unsheathe a bowie knife or draw his revolver. He, however, evidently felt the influence of civilized surroundings too strongly to indulge in such playfully wild habits.

His conversation was highly flavored with slang and profanity. His manners were as uncouth as his appearance was startling. His voice was an admixture of nasal twang and brutal grunt.

Although he seemed the embodiment of a rough, dangerous element, sometimes found in distant mining territories, where savage habits had long since obliterated all traces of early parental teaching and civilized custom, yet, with his flowing locks thrown back from an intellectual forehead, his classic features, an athletic figure and a costume which might be copied for its effect by the star stage brigand, Joe Jungle was, in his mining home, a picture not easily forgotten.

His partners had gradually dropped out, leaving only two quiet gentlemen, Lord Fitzgerald, an Irishman, and Lord Oakdale, an Englishman. Nevertheless, the Wayback never ceased to curse the British and in the same manner consign the Irish to the bottom of Hades.

Lord Oakdale and his companion were amused beyond measure. To them this indigenous plant of the primitive West far exceeded anything ever witnessed in Barnum's "Consolidated Circus" or Buffalo Bill's "Wild West."

They were so delighted with the *rara avis*, they not only smiled at his rude sayings, but egged him on at the slightest suspicion of the conversation terminating. Although not an expert at poker, Lord Fitzgerald won a game.

"Gol durn my pictur'," said Jungle, "I don't care a cuss fur the dust, but I'm bleowed ef I want a durned Irishman to beat a' American from wayback." After awhile the Wayback won every game, no one seemed to have the slightest chance against him. Finally Lord Fitzgerald withdrew, leaving Lord Oakdale to again be finished by the proficient Westerner.

"I tell you," hawhawed Wayback, "it

does me good to wollop a' Englisher. I hate the impodunt Irish, but I'll be bleowed ef I don't b'lieve I'd jine 'em to lick the stuckup English. They think they're the only ones top o' earth fit ter live; keowards all of um. They'd run from a hen-fight ef they heard a wing flap."

"Where," questioned Lord Oakdale, striving to suppress a smile, "did you meet my countrymen?"

"Never see many on um 'fore you, but I've heard of um, an' I never want to see 'nother. Ef I had a' American steamer to shoot me over th' Atlantic Ocean next week, I wouldn't ride in no English Cullard steamer, you bet; but neow I've got tew, I s'pose, to git ter Glasgow, as thar' ain't no b'loons I ken take passage in 'stead of a British gol durned salt water express. Hope I won't meet no English lords on the ship, anyway.

"I'll play ye 'nother game ef ye like to be wolloped," and the Wayback opened a jackpot containing $500.

Lord Oakdale squeezed down his hand, and raised the opener with aces and kings.

Another raise came from Wayback, who held three queens, and who was again raised by Lord Oakdale. Then cards were drawn, Lord Oakdale drawing one and the Wayback drawing two.

Betting now went fast and furious. Nothing could be heard but the click of the chips, and the excitement rose to fever heat, until the pot reached $5,000. Lord Oakdale called, the hands were exposed. Lord Oakdale had an ace full on kings, and the Wayback four queens.

As Joe Jungle raked in the money and added to his wad of bills, he chuckled: " Wall, I've hed some fun anyheow, lickin' the English an' Irish. Gol durn um, they ain't fit ter live, anyway. Keowards all of um," and again he expectorated tobacco juice, like a fall of rain, over and around the cuspidor.

At this point a young rector leisurely entered. In a moment the Wayback seemed ready to challenge the newcomer to mortal combat, but finally lay back in his chair and sneered:

"A gosh durned parson on the train, I'll be bleowed! Say, boys, we'll have a smash-up! Parson, what's yer name and whar' do you come from, anyheow?"

The rector caught a peculiar look from his friends Oakdale and Fitzgerald, and concluded to reply to the insolent Wayback.

"My name, sir," responded the rector, with most amiable politeness, "is Royal Wadsworth, and my place of birth Irela——"

"Git out!" interrupted Wayback. "I might o' knowed it, nothin' reound me ever sence this car left Deadwood but gol durned English an' Irish tourists. An' then a parson aboard! We'll roll over a Rocky Mountain precipice. Parsons!" he disgustingly repeated. "No good on airth, keowards all of um. Goin' reound tellin' 'beout a God somewhar', as ef folks didn't know better'n ter believe anything they ken't see, nur handle, nur git tew.

"That's what that 'ere feller says that writ the 'Mistakes uv the Almighty,' an' I'd ruther b'lieve him a durned sight, fer I have seen Wongersol, en' shook hands with him, an' laffed, an' laffed hearin' him tell his Bible jokes, but I ain't onct see th' Almighty.

"Jess ez Wongersol says, we've been gulled tew long, talkin' to a God who pertends He knows mor'n we du. Good 'nuff pap fur women an' childurn, but fur men to b'lieve in a God—shew! Its played eout!

"As Wongersoll says, says he, "Ef thar was a God he'd tell us everything, an' not go sneakin' 'reound buildin' a heavenly home for us in some country we don't know nothin' 'beout, whether its swampy or rocky, an' maybe wouldn't agree with us if we got thar'. May be full of malary, an' then perposin' to never let us see the inside on't till arter we're dead like a dog. What's the good of it then, I'd like to know?

"De ye s'pose ef thar' wuz a God he wouldn't let us live allers? 'Taint likely neow He'd put us miserable roosters here jess ter stay a few fleetin' years an' then let us die. No, He'd never be so cussed mean as that, so I've concluded with Wongersol, of York, that thar' ain't no God 'tall, ur He'd told us all that was goin' on, every 'tarnal thing He intended doin' fur us and let us know jess ez much ez He does.

"Why, instead of killin' us and puttin' us in the ground ter rot, He'd take us to t'other home in a balloon and at half th' expense. Ez fur me, I'll be gol durned ef I wouldn't a good sight ruther go that way," and he again expectorated tobacco rain.

"Naw, sir-ee, ye ken't tell me that He'd chuck our bodies in the greound ter rot an' take our speerit er our soul a-soarin' away on a picnic inter heaven to git a new body fit ter 'sociate with stuckup angels.

"That may du fur crowned heads, who allers want great paradin' over themselves, but I b'long to a free Republic, an' my old, sarviceable body, that's been yanked 'reound with me through thick and thin, ain't goin' to be throwed away fur no newfangled ghost apparatus arter I'm dead.

"Ef thar wuz a God he'd see that jess as well ez me an' Wongersoll an' other sharp-eyed inferdels see it.

"A parson! Jess guess human natur' ken paddle her own canoe without no parson.

"Most on 'em come 'reound a commoonity a-sticken' their noses inter ever'body's private business, a-tryin' to reform drunkards an' sich like, an objectin' to people gittin' a livin' by runnin' games of draw pcker that's a good place fur fellars without brains to lose their money in, but what stuckups call gamblin'.

"I knowed one decent parson, though. He come around tew camp 'bout year ago. Wanted ter sprinkle water on Hank's head. I told him ter keep off. I didn't want no baptizin' reound him, nur no gosh durned parson's hand to tech him nuther.

"Then the parson tried ter tell me what baptizin' meant, and sponsor. Sez he, 'Ye know, Meester Jungle, ef ye wuz goin' to die, ye'd want some good friend afore it was tew late—a' honest man—tew promise he'd look after yer children and see that they was brought up honest and edicated, a guardian jess ez execeters is left fur estates.

"'Now, then, 'twouldn't be 'nuff ter satisfy ye fur the execeter ter send ye word he'd kerry out yer wishes an' do ever'thing squar'.

He'd have ter go through a form o' law en give bonds, tew.

"'Now, a sponsor does jess the same by takin' a vow that a child shell be brought up in the religion of his parents, reverence a divine Father, and not be raised in inferdelity.'

"'Now, then,' says I, 'that's jess what I don't want l'arned him—no life beyond the grave and sich stuff.

"'Hank's goin' to be a' eout an' eout inferdel, like me an' Wongersol, of York. No foolin' 'beout it nuther.

"'So git yer baptizin' tools, Bible, water an' all, eouter this ranch quick ez lightnin', er the fust thing ye know ye'll be ornamentin' the limb uv a tree that I keep growed fur that purpose. I give ye ten minutes afore I come back.'

"Well, what d'ye think the gol durned fool done, but flopped right deown an' went to talkin' to God 'beout me, an' I left him prayin'. Jess then Hank come by the door an' listened. Hank never see a circus afore, so I thought I'd let him an' the Chinaman have a free ticket ter see th' elephant.

"Arter awhile I sneaked back, an' ef thar wa'n't Hank kneelin' with the parson, an' the parson was larnin' him the Lord's prayer. An' thar was Hank goin' it fer all he was wo'th—jess as ef he wa'n't a' inferdel—an' finished up with what Jennie, his dead mother, l'arned him, 'Neow I lay me deown ter sleep.'"

Here the Wayback coughed and his voice did not seem quite so boisterous, not quite, but he continued:

"Then Hank said suthin' 'beout, 'Lord bless pop, an' all the miners an' their fam'lies. May pop live ter take care o' me and see me grow up a good man.' The parson said, 'Amen, my boy,' an' put his religi's hand, lovin'-like, right on Hank's head.

"Afore I knowed it I had yanked off my hat jess ez ef I wuz in a meetin'-house.'

"I wuz so mad, a tear jess dropped on my cheek. Suthin' kind o' swelled up in my throat till I felt ez if I had the mumps, but I coughed it away.

"I was so mad I went in kind o' soft like, en I says, 'Parson, the tree I hang parsons on ez cut deown, an' I hain't got no time to hunt 'nother, an' I guess yer feet is wet. I wish you'd take this tew hundurd dollars wo'th o' gold eagles, an' git away quick fur a new pa'r o' boots.

"I'm awful mad, fur ye know I'm a' inferdel, an' wet feet is a dangerous thing this weather. What a fool I wuz, parson, not ter notice yer boots afore; that kind o' leather allers soaks water, 'specially ef it's worn till holes git in.'

"Then I shook hands with him, an' says, 'Good-bye.' I wuz so mad.

"The parson's eyes looked kind o' red an' weak, and ez he took the money an' shook hands ag'in, he trembled all over an' couldn't speak. I s'pose he wuz mad tew.

"Then he took Hank in his arms an' kissed him, an' I let him do it. Then he said suthin' 'beout meetin' me in our Father's house, after this brief life wuz over. An' I shook hands ag'in with him, an' stood with my hat off. I wuz so thunderin' mad.

"Arter he started, Hank called arter him to 'come ag'in,' an' he called back, 'I will, my boy, Providence permittin', in tew weeks.' I didn't say nuthin' ag'in it; I thought I'd jess as soon he'd come back ez not.

"Arter he'd gone, I wuz so mad somehow, I couldn't go ter work, So I jess took Hank right in my arms an' got onter a high rock an' watched that poor, foolish, good-nater'd parson clean out o' sight.

"Poor fellar, he took cold by them bust-out old boots, durn 'em, jess ez I wuz 'fraid of, an' died in one week at the next ranch.

"The two hundurd he divided 'twixt his family in the East and a little church he was a tryin' to build in the minin' deestrick.

"I sent his poor body home to his wife with a ten thousand check pinned on the parson's coat collar fur funeral 'xpenses, an' writ her she'd never want fur nothin' while Joe Jungle lived.

"I allers feel kind o' glad to know I give the parson that tew hundurd fur noo boots, though the poor parson never lived to wear um.

"The boots wuz like the very last words he talked ter me, they come 'tew late.'"

Joe Jungle stared into vacancy, while those present looked at the Wayback with a new and kindly interest. Lord Oakdale was the first to break the silence.

"Mr. Jungle, may I beg to know to whom you refer as 'Hank'?"

In a moment the face of the Wayback was radiant, his voice dropped to a tender cadence, and pointing to a chair he softly replied, "Thar's my Hank."

A sweet boy of about seven years lay asleep in a chair, his little chu'by hands clasping a woolly horse, which was hugged to his bosom. His dimpled cheeks were rosy with health's fresh beauty.

The long dark lashes swept his lovely face as though vying for admiration, while from the wearily reclining head fell fluffy curls of silken gold.

No monarch ever gazed upon his first-born heir with such proud rapture as did

this idolizing father at his darling boy. The rector quietly looked, while the other gentlemen expressed their admiration of the beautiful child.

Pen could not picture the pride, the depth of love which shone in the face of the infidel Joe Jungle, as he unconsciously, reverently whispered, "My Hank, God bless him!"

The rector grasped the hand of the Wayback, and feelingly responded, "Amen! And may the child lead the parent!"

CHAPTER II.

ONE VICTIM.

"BUT, darling, why use the coarsest mode of expression?"

"My dear," responded Mrs. Rodney's husband, "I believe in calling things by their proper names.

"I did not study medicine two years and not know that the subcutaneous penetralia, which penetrates the precipitous infundibuliform of the culdesac, causes belly-a——"

"Don't say that again!" screamingly interrupted Aunt Sophronie. "The Rodney intellect always overtops just a 'leetle,' but, Nell, that wretch" (looking good-naturedly at her nephew) "only drew you into this silly argument to air his Æsculapian knowledge. He knows perfectly that stomach-ache is more euphonious than" (hesitating)—"than the other word, and sufficiently expressive for anyone not a student of *materia medica.*"

"Oh, certainly, aunt," smiled Mr. Rodney, "only this straining a point in mock modesty was suggested by Miss Pinkley, who told us last evening of the terrible accident to her uncle's 'limb,' which had been amputated.

"Without further inquiry, we were in a perfect state of ignorance as to whether it was a leg or an arm which had been surgeonized, and when that girl had to admit it was a *leg* she looked as though she had committed all the crimes in the calendar.

"I thought what delicious inconsistency, when the mother of this same girl, who teaches her daughter such absurd nonsense, which no doubt she religiously believes the acme of modesty, will deck her child, whom I have seen in a dress exposing nearly all her upper body, and allow her to spin around a ball-room, hugged up to a mere acquaintance, whose money or family has probably saved his expulsion from decent society.

"Or, she may whirl in the arms of an utter stranger immediately after he is presented to her.

"It is but a short time since fashionable mothers of our own country generally began to appreciate the fact that it was, to say the least, in extremely bad taste to send off a daughter to balls with an escort, who, after dancing to enchanting music, takes her to supper, where she partakes of wine, which flies to her head, and drives home again with the man, who probably has now much more of the intoxicant in his brain than the charming creature by his side. And this is still practiced by some women who call it 'independence of character.'"

"Well," replied Mrs. Rodney, "though the man's reputation were immaculate, I should consider such habits, with that of hugging to music, to say the least, not calculated to enhance the delicacy of a properly brought up woman."

"You have it, my dear," said Mr. Rodney.

"'Hugging to music' is a correct name for the waltz, a dance which, as conducted even in our best society, is only fitted for unmentionable places.

"Relegate the waltz to relatives or most intimate friends only, and it would speedily lose its fascination.

"We piously refer to the degradation of woman in Mohammedan countries, believing that they veil their faces from men only to hide a shame. We send missionaries to convert them to Christianity, to whom one of their first women read this lesson :

"'See! Is this a real picture of your waltz, where mothers, wives, daughters, throw themselves into the arms of different men?'

"The missionary was compelled to admit its truth. Then said she :

"'Return to your respectable waltzers, tell them they are the heathen—not we. Nor dare insult us by comparison with your females. May Allah curse your mothers and their offspring, for such vulgar, degrading habits.'

"Imagine the feelings of our Christian missionary.

"Bah!

"A mere speaking acquaintance taking your mother, wife, daughter or sweetheart in his arms, and making several hugging tours of a ball-room, accompanied by strains of entrancing music, the *music*, of course, supposed to *sanctify* the *hugging!*

"Fiji Islanders could not be guilty of more immodesty. Even the Shah, when first visiting England, could not understand our waltz for refined society, and offered to buy several of the women thus engaged. When told they were the wives and daughters of those who had assembled to honor him, the Shah laughingly replied:

"'You think that is a very good joke on me. No, no; the women are professional dancers, and strong too, very strong. I have noticed some of them whirl with a dozen different men to-night, and seem ready to embrace as many more. See! see! Yes, I will buy twenty. They shall amuse my soldiers with that amazingly refined ball-room exercise, from the country of the Christian.' And the Shah leered a subtle sneer."

"As a little girl," responded Mrs. Rodney, "I was wild to waltz. Aside from being a clergyman, my father was strictly opposed to all dancing, while my mother objected only to waltzing. One day she told me of Miss Sherman, daughter of General Sherman, a Roman Catholic, who, being honored by the Prince of Wales' request for a waltz, at the reception of welcome to him here, sweetly declined by replying, 'Waltzing is against the rules of my Church.'

"The Prince bowed, admiringly, and courteously stood by her side until the close of the objectionable measure, when Miss Sherman, with unaffected pleasure, accepted the arm of the Prince and glided into the graceful quadrille.

"Happy mother! proud Church to have such a daughter! I was so charmed with Miss Sherman's act, it caused me to consider my mother's objections, and checked all further desire for waltzing."

"Nell, dear, if you had been a waltzer I never would have done myself the honor of asking you to become Mrs. Rodney. I vowed I would not marry a woman who was in the habit of being publicly hugged."

"Well, my dear nephew," exclaimed Aunt Sophronie, "how about men?"

"My dear aunt, it is true men declare themselves privileged in doing what they will not grant your sex. But I admit that women have the right to expect and demand the same purity in men that we expect and demand in women, and until society takes this stand it will continue to be what it is—a rotten composition.

"Very bitter doses were those administered from our best pulpits lately, and the great nausea they occasioned clearly showed the unmistakable need of the cleansing purgative."

"Amen to them," responded Aunt Sophronie. "I will go to my room at once and attack a poem on the subject of waltzing. I feel the inspiration now, the real divine afflatus," and away she sped.

Will Darrow, an intimate friend of Ned Rodney's, now appeared at the library door looking deathly pale. Mr. Rodney sprang toward him. "What is it, Will? Anything the matter? Sit down, you look ready to faint."

"I called to say," replied young Darrow, "that I could not keep my engagement with you to-day. A great sorrow has fallen upon our home. Sister Bess has eloped with John Walton."

The Rodneys looked aghast.

"Ned," said Darrow, "I always made light of your objection to waltzing, but that degrading familiarity has stolen the senses of my only sister. Last night I called to bring her from the subscription ball, when I learned she had disappeared with Walton, to whom I had forbidden her to speak, but he managed to have her waltz with him, and this is the result. I fear my mother will die. I must go to her. Good-bye," and Darrow rushed out, looking the picture of insanity.

Mr. Rodney drew a long breath and indignantly remarked:

"So much for society's respectable measure, 'the hugging waltz.' Poor Bess is henceforth an outcast.

"But mark the villain. Before a twelvemonth society will open its arms to him, and he will be considered the more charming to have had so exciting a romance as the degrading of a respectable woman. The higher she stands the more valuable the conquest for this fascinating *roué*."

Mrs. Rodney's face looked her indignation.

"Never will any respectable family allow that monster to enter their home again."

"Ah, my dear," said Mr. Rodney, "you are not aware that the 'monster' has an income of thirty or forty thousand per annum, with additional prospects from his old uncle. He is considered one of the best catches.

"The first time Walton enters church, after his return, you will see half the women glance from their prayer-books to get a look at the 'splendid man who so foolishly permitted himself to be ensnared (?).'"

Mrs. Rodney moaned: "Oh, poor girl! How could she crush her family and ruin her life?"

"Simply because there is poison in the atmosphere of the modern ball-room," replied Mr. Rodney. "Like deathly contagion it may not inoculate all; through some phlegmatic natures it may never penetrate; but I challenge any man who has had experience as a waltzer to truthfully deny that, indulged in to any extent, it does not finally turn the tide between friends, sweethearts, husbands and wives, until they are swept to the seething whirlpool, from which the voice of affection is powerless to recall.

"Here is an article I noticed this morning," and Mr. Rodney produced one of the dailies.

"WALTZING.

"THE SENATE OF GEORGIA SAYS THAT THE CHRISTIAN PULPIT IS AGAINST IT, AND THE CITIZENS OF THE STATE LIKEWISE.

"Senator McCarty arose to speak.

"'I agree with the amendment (in the celebration at the completion of the State Capitol). Every church in the land stands up against it. The issue was tried in a church in Atlanta years ago, and great confusion resulted from it. Many good people dance, but few waltz, and when you go down to the solid, cultured people of Georgia, they protest against this use of the Capitol. The churches endeavor to keep up to what they conceive to be a standard of purest sentiment, and here we are invited by resolution to turn the Capitol over to that which every pulpit, whenever occasion offers, is speaking against, and sincerely against.

"'I do not believe it is right to turn the Capitol of Georgia into a modern ball-room. How many ministers of Atlanta, who are striving to support the principles of religion, would come here and take part in waltzing. Their standard and the sentiments cherished by them are better than any amendment the world has made so far. Our best people, the Christian churches have spoken against this all over Georgia, and it is time the Senate should speak now.'

"The amendment was adopted."

"I think it quite time to draw halt, when dancing, from its primitive, beautiful simplicity, has reached a point where we can calmly gaze upon mothers, wives, daughters in a debasing waltz! now lolling in a man's arms, of the most formal acquaintance; anon, hugged to his breast.

"It is the strangest enactment countenanced by a respectable people."

Mr. Rodney stopped short, and sighed, "Poor Bess!"

Mrs. Rodney clasped her hands, and with tears in her voice, muttered, "Dear girl! Lost! lost! Heaven pity her!"

CHAPTER III.

DISCUSSING THE WALTZ.

MR. RODNEY, going toward the window, remarked:

"Who is that coming up the walk? Mrs. Vaintone. She comes to save a trip to my office. A client I should not regret to lose. She was once very friendly with Walton, in fact gossip had it they were 'engaged,' but she suddenly married Jim Vaintone."

"May I come in?" beseeched a female voice at the library door, a moment later, and a sallow, unpleasant face peeped in.

"Come in," said Mrs. Rodney. "Delightful weather."

"Charming!" responded Mrs. Vaintone.

"The weather has lent some of its loveliness to one of its adorers," said Mr. Rodney. "I suppose you desire to attest those papers, but they are not ready."

"Oh, well, it is no matter," replied Mrs. Vaintone. "How are the twins?"

"Well, and mischievous as squirrels," responded Mrs. Rodney. "Roby is here one moment and in the top of a tree the next. Ruby is almost his equal in climbing. She doesn't care for dolls, and seems to enjoy only her brother's boyish sports. I despair of ever refining her."

"Never mind, my dear," suggested Mr. Rodney; "time enough for that process. If you would have perfect loveliness in the inceptive flower, give it air, light, freedom. Sweet, short-lived bud too soon to blossom. Her romps, my dear, will never generate seeds of weakness, rest assured."

"Papa, this dawg wont haave hisself," said Roby, dragging his dog Rover by a chain; "him keeps pullin' and pullin'."

As Roby stood in the room Mr. Rodney took the chain, saying, "My son, you are very rude; you have not spoken to Mrs. Vaintone."

"Well," replied Roby, curtly, "I seed her when I comed in."

"But, my dear," rebuked his mother, "*seeing* a lady or gentleman is not sufficient. Be polite and speak to Mrs. Vaintone."

Roby reluctantly pulled off his hat, and looking very downcast, approached the repugnant visitor.

"Good morning, Roby," said Mrs. Vaintone; "when are you coming to visit us?"

Roby looked her straight in the face and answered, "I don't comin' ober to youm houth any mo'."

"Why not?" asked Mrs. Vaintone, with most wounded emphasis.

"Coth why," replied Roby, working his mouth to get around the big words, "I licked youm boy lath time I went to youm houth."

"Oh!" exclaimed Roby's parents. "How shocking; why did you commit such a dreadful act?"

"Well," drawled out Roby, "Jim kicked my dawg, and Ruby tole him not to do so no more. Den him called her twom-bwoy, and she cwied; then I strucked him gude."

Ruby, who had been at the door, peeking

through, rushed in to defend her brother's courageous act.

"Yeth, and brover tole Jim if he eber call me twom-bwoy agin, he would lick him worther."

And both children danced, in high glee at the remembrance of the justly inflicted punishment meted out to the child of the lady before them.

"Son," said Mrs. Rodney, striving to look serious, "this is something too dreadful. Strike a playfellow? Apologize to Mrs. Vaintone at once, and tell her you will never be guilty of such an outrageous act again."

Roby shrugged his shoulders, as though non-inclined to make concession, but sidling up, began:

"I is sowy I licked Jim, an' I won't do it agin, leth he kicks my dawg, or calls sister 'twom-bwoy.' Then if him do, I'll lick him worther."

Delivering the last sentence with clenched fists and flashing eye, he grasped Ruby's hand and before his astounded auditors could recover their equipoise had cleared the house.

"Oh, no, don't call him back," laughed Mrs. Vaintone. "I would give anything to see so much spirit in Jim, but he never did take after me."

Mr. Rodney, who had been enjoying the scene, now offered an apology for his son by referring to his very tender affection for his sister and his dog Rover.

"There, again, he is unlike Jim," said Mrs. Vaintone. "The boys might exhaust their vocabulary of epithets on *his* sister, and he would never move a muscle in her defense.

"The same difference in children as in men and women.

"By the way, did you know that foolish Walton had gone off with Bess Darrow?"

"'Foolish Walton!'" savagely remarked Mr. Rodney; "*devilish* Walton, you mean. He had better forever keep out of Will Darrow's path or that brother will resent his sister's outrage with death!"

"I very much fear so," responded Mrs. Rodney.

"What nonsense," said Mrs. Vaintone, "to attempt to defend that young hussy, or visit her crime on the temporarily infatuated man whom she inveigled!"

"Ah," observed Mrs. Rodney, "then you are one of those who deny forgiveness to your own sex, but uphold and pet a profligate, whose chief occupation of his manhood, or malehood, has been to destroy homes and blast the lives of his betrayed victims."

"He is utterly harmless if checked in time," smilingly responded Mrs. Vaintone. "The great fascination for Bess Darrow seemed to rest in Walton's exquisite waltzing."

"Ha!" sneered Mr. Rodney; "a respectable woman lolling and spinning around a ball-room, to music, in the arms of a mere acquaintance; or, in other words, submitting to being publicly hugged by a variety of men——"

"Oh!" interrupted Mrs. Vaintone. "We are not hugged—we are only steadied by the man's arm."

"Steadied!" repeated Mr. Rodney, savagely. "Pardon me. Before I married, I was ten years in society; danced at all the fashionable houses; attended every swell ball; and no matter how dignifiedly my partner started out in the round dances, nine cases out of ten she became so dizzy that long before we finished her head, of necessity, reclined on my bosom.

"I have a friend who will not invite a certain man to his own home because of his character, yet at any fashionable reception his wife and daughters may be found hugging to music the same *roué.*

"You smile," continued Mr. Rodney, as a peculiar acknowledgment broke over the face of Mrs. Vaintone, who was indolently eyeing him from under her drooping lashes, "because you know that I speak simple *facts.*"

"Oh, dear," said Mrs. Vaintone, "some men fancy the whole world revolves around their ideal of womanhood, which is, of course, at first, their wives, and whatever they do must be perfect. Mrs. Rodney does not waltz, but she dresses *décolleté*. I wonder you do not object to *that*."

"On the contrary, I very much favor a lady's modest evening toilet ; and I consider it woman's duty to adorn herself most becomingly, but I believe the beautiful neck and arms should be admired as something of our Creator's most perfect work, and as sacred from vulgar, public hugging as a defenseless Venus would be from the profane dragging off her pedestal."

"You must admit," said Mrs. Vaintone, "that waltzing has been made a great success."

"Success!" sneeringly repeated Mr. Rodney. "Well, I will not question your intelligence, while that word is so misapplied.

"Is the play a 'success'? is a work of art a 'success'? is the politician a 'success'? money or the vulgar majority homogeneously now decide.

"The dramatic representative who rants, strides, outrages every artistic feeling, may ride roughshod over the intensely real, natural, conscientious artist, because a vulgar majority gawpingly cries 'Success!'

"The author who insinuates the greatest amount of defiling filth sails peacefully and wealthily over those whose heart and soul shine through their work, in striving to lift mankind to purer atmosphere, because the majority make it a 'success.'

"Our critics, who may be born Ruskins, sensitively refined, acutely appreciative, who have devoted a lifetime to delving in the richest bejeweled literary and artistic mines, are 'poohpoohed' against the opinion of illiterate jackanapes, who are usually in the majority, and applaudingly scream 'Success!'

"Here in New York I heard an atheist declare to thousands of listeners, in ridicule of simple history, that he did not 'believe such a man as Jesus Christ ever lived.'

"This speaker possessed exceptional talents, and for these gifts expressed his gratitude by sneering at the existence of a Supreme Creator.

"Hearts of hundreds were palsied who

fancied themselves at their mother's knee, devoutly lisping their first innocent thanksgiving, 'Our Father who art in heaven,' yet the laugh, stamp and screech of the majority echoed 'Success!'

"We have had ages given over to religious worship, hero worship, art worship; but this age must certainly be transmitted to posterity as the worship of 'success,' most of the success being defined by quantity *versus* quality.

"Thus, also, is the debasing waltz a 'success.'

"Nine-tenths," continued Mr. Rodney, "of our girl debutantes are now, by their parents, given a "hugging to music" ball as the proper thing in which to launch their modest, uninitiated daughter on the sea of fashionable society, thus teaching her, as the sequel proves, to forget as speedily as possible the good she may have learned, as being of no earthly value in comparison to the latest step in dancing and the perfection of the 'enchanting waltz,' which latter means being promiscuously pressed to the bosoms of men, even as an affectionate husband would take his beloved wife in his arms for a welcome embrace.

"Does not one-half the blame belong to women who thus stimulate men's baser passions by enfolding them in the waltz?

"We are like you, flesh and blood, but lack woman's spirituality, which curbs the inborn sensuousness.

"I am not shielding my own sex, but this very predominating animalism will, under alluring circumstances, cause many an honorable man to forget that he should stand toward womanhood in the same light as the family physician who attended her first earthly cry, or her pastor, who held her in his arms at the baptismal font and blessed her.

"Does it belong to the mission of a good woman to inflame with her ravishing incense, to basely intoxicate with her angelic form pulsating in a man's arms, with only the excuse of 'music' for this mutual hugging?

"We hear of ballet girls who modestly shrink from their first short waists and skirts in which they are decked to complete a picture, and to that end are compelled to submit.

"Fashionable mothers and daughters in the audience gasp a little 'Oh!' of shocked (?) vision, while they peek through the gauze of their fans to obtain a better view.

"The next night finds the latter in a ballroom with their upper bodies exposed to a degree which would be reprimanded by the stage manager of any respectable theater, and in which aforesaid indelicate garb they are, as usual, promiscuously hugging men to music.

"The warm season comes. A public beach this time is used to advertise the lower portion of their bodies and for the edification of the multitude.

"These are not compulsory exhibitions for a weekly salary, which often to the ballet girl means the sole support of an invalid mother or dependent family. Oh, no! theirs is a nobler (?) ambition.

"They are seeking bids for vanity's admiration or a golden husband, whose home with them in the future will be a society hotel, managed solely for the entertainment of this same class, wherein to discuss the latest german and arrange anew for their enchanting waltz.

"If the husband's business goes wrong, let him bear his burden alone, nor dare to expect that his wife will dispense with another new toilet for the next ball, nor in his longing heart dare to wish from her one sympathizing word, one encouraging caress.

"If children—whom she unwillingly bore—are ill, they have nurses. Would you ask such a woman to sacrifice a 'hugging to music' evening for the sick room?

"No! no! The maddening whirl is the life she craves, and will have, even at the cost of wifely or motherhood's most sacred duties."

"Well," sing-songed Mrs. Vaintone, "suppose the husband is the waltzer."

"If the husband is the 'hugger to music,' then the wife is left at home to bear the burdens of life alone.

"And when both husband and wife are

carried away with this base passion, their life declines to a give-and-take sort of partnership, where affection between them becomes a thing to sneer at as 'too tame' for home indulgence."

Mrs. Vaintone winced, but recalling herself, lazily drawled out the worn and senseless apothegm:

"To the pure all things are pure."

"Which, in this sense," scathingly replied Mr. Rodney, "is like the man in the Western restaurant who remarked to the waiter:

"'This glass of water smells as though it had seeped through a graveyard.'

"'Yas, sah,' said the waiter, 'it do run through a graveyard, sah, but it is de most respectablest cemintary in de city, sah, and de richest corpses is buried dar.'

"So, if respectable people decide to indulge in immodesty, the act must be considered modest. Pure impurity is indeed no more an anomaly than that *fashion* rectifies immorality, or that coarsest vulgarity, once entered in the kaleidoscope of society, is metamorphosed into the most chaste refinement."

"Then you," said Mrs. Vaintone, languidly moving, "hold waltzing responsible for all the misfortunes which blur our fashionable escutcheon?"

"There are other extremes which cause misery beside waltzing; but what I mean is briefly this, and in which I am supported by the clergy and cultured people of the Christian world:

"Be she wife, mother or maid, decked out in fashionable array, which means, at the present time, half her upper body exposed, lolling in the arms of strangers or men who are mere acquaintances, her partially nude, throbbing bosoms pressed to her partner, and hugging to music around a ball-room, is the most indecent, barbarous inconsistency for a civilized, respectable people of the nineteenth century."

Moral dancing manners of our great-great-grandparents. (Page 50.)

Improved moral (?) dancing manners—Hugging to Music—performed by some of their great-great-grandchildren. (Page 50.)

CHAPTER IV.

THE BALL.

THE night of the Asvanterlet reception had arrived. Aunt Sophronie, with paper and pencil in hand, sat in a conservatory just off the ball-room, occasionally condescending to look, in utter disgust, at the modern fashionable measures. She was folding a long manuscript as Charles Deluth, one of the worst *roués*, whose money alone had saved his expulsion from decent society, entered, evidently in quest of some one beside Miss Sophronie Rodney.

"Ah," thought he, "Miss Rodney, a relative of the charming Mrs. Lennox. I must flatter the spinster some way, but haven't an idea what her little weakness is. Well, first I will ask her to waltz. It will be a dreadful penance, but here goes," as he strode up to her, and waited until the blue spectacles turned full upon him. Deluth bowed low and with his most winning smile exchanged the compliments of the evening, after which he most graciously asked:

"Miss Rodney, will you honor me with the next waltz?"

Aunt Sophronie Rodney grew inches taller in a moment, as she replied: "Waltz with you? Did I understand you asked me to waltz?"

Deluth smiled despite himself as he replied: "Yes, Miss Rodney, I beg that pleasure."

"Well, now," said Aunt Sophronie as she tipped back with indignation, "why don't you speak plain English and ask me to hug you?"

Deluth looked ready to faint.

"Yes," continued she, "hug you to music, that's what it is, pure and simple. A potato is a potato, and calling it a peach can't alter its shape or change its flavor. There, look at 'em," as several couples waltzed by the door. "What would you call that if you had me in your arms fifteen or twenty minutes without the music?"

"Oh, dreadful!" exclaimed Deluth, so suspiciously quick that Aunt Sophronie looked up, but he regained his composure and ventured a reply.

"My dear Miss Rodney, there are some situations, though ever so carefully considered and arranged, which will appear, you see, to certain eyes and minds, not in unison with its poetic tendency, and thus involve a contact inharmonious to the uninitiated."

"Poetic tendency," repeated Aunt Sophronie, who seemed willing to tolerate even Deluth if he was poetically inclined. "I wonder now if you write poetry?"

Deluth had discovered her weakness, and hastily replied: "Oh, a very little, but I am very fond of those gifted in that direction. I have heard you spoken of as a poetic genius. I trust you will sometime grant me the happiness of hearing a selection of your celebrated effusions."

"Why, if you wouldn't mind," said she, "taking one in your pocket on 'Waltzing,' you can have this one," and she proceeded to draw forth a fearful manuscript from her huge pocket, much to the consternation of Deluth. "You see, I write whenever the inspiration seizes me, and I was seized that way to-night while waiting for my niece, Vic Lennox. Wonder she is not here yet.

"A poet, like school teaching or any other art, requires a great deal of practice.

"I know I possess talent for poetry from the reams of it I used to write at school; but I seemed to have always lacked inspiration for just what I wished to say at the particular moment.

"I sometimes miss, as my teacher used to tell me, the 'divine afflatus.' She always insisted that was all I lacked to make a renowned poetess; otherwise, I could write reams and reams of matter."

Anxious for the good opinion of Mrs. Lennox's relative, Deluth quickly replied:

"Do let me hear what you have written," and he endeavored to return the objectionable roll of manuscript.

"Oh, no," said Aunt Sophronie, "you can keep that one on hugging to music; in respectable society it is termed waltzing.

"I have another here just begun, to my dear nephew and niece. To-morrow will be the darlings' birthday; so I thought it appropriate to write a little poem in commemoration. I don't seem to get along very rapidly, though."

"Ah," replied Deluth, "those charming little twins merit a place in poetic history. Something descriptive will be delightful for them to have in later years. Proceed, dear Miss Rodney."

Aunt Sophronie, now thoroughly conscious of her poetic importance, began:

"To my darling nephew and niece, the twins
"ROBY and RUBY,
"By their loving aunt, Sophronie Rodney.

"Each little twin,
Tucked in a bin,
oid of all sin——

"I haven't got very far. Now you will kind o' help me out, won't you? I wish this a surprise to their parents."

"It will indeed be a surprise. As to helping you, my dear Miss Rodney, your genius is altogether too deep for me to be of the slightest assistance."

Aunt Sophronie was radiant.

"Ah, how lovely of you to see that I possess talent for poetry, although it is latent."

"Yes," replied Deluth, "some talents are always 'latent.' And I would advise you not to weary yourself just now. Too profound, you see. Something lighter would be better; not so wearing on the intellect.

"To think," responded Aunt Sophronie, "how, in future years, those two cherubs will prize this poem of their childhood, written by their aunt—of course with a little assistance from you——"

"No, no, dear Miss Rodney. I would not rob you of such merited fame. That your poem is entirely and absolutely your own will be apparent to all. '*Poeta nascitar non fit*,' you know; 'Nature, not study, forms the poet.'

"You see, my life has been wasted in the dry confines of business. Genius, in me, never had time to develop. An average rationality carried me through college. I even won distinction in that dry laboratory. But to think of poetry never entered my wildest projects.

"Talent and wit such as yours, dear Miss Rodney, hath been denied me. I am only a poor plodder, utterly void of that transcendental exercitation for the immense deliberation, deep consideration, quick speculation and thoughtful cogitation necessary to the gifted cerebration which holds consultation and turns the wheel of the imagination."

"Ah, that is so like my dear nephew, Ned Rodney," exclaimed Aunt Sophronie, while paper and pencil flew east and west. "I always said he had the clearest judgment and appreciation—the only one of the Rodneys who takes after me. The dull brain of my other relatives could never understand why I always so strongly took to him.

"'There,' said I, 'is a man with a penetration worthy of an Aristotle; an Herculean mind, possessing heaven-given power of expressing his sentiments in language befitting the most learned men of the dark ages.'

"'Was I wrong in making my will in

favor of my dearest nephew? No; and when I am laid to rest, the weeping willow waving o'er my grassy mound, as it were, then will he know that his Aunt Sophronie appreciated his mammoth intellect, even though heaven hath denied him, as he regrettingly admits, the genius of a Byronic poet;" and gathering up her scattered utensils Aunt Sophronie resumed the reading.

"Two little twins,
  Tucked in their bins,
  Free from all sins
  Of our flesh and fins —"

"Ah!" gasped Deluth, "too fishy for the human family. Fins, Miss Rodney, will never do."

"Well, give me some word for fins—the 'flesh' is all right, isn't it?"

Deluth was compelled to admit that the Rodney twins were presumably of the Rodney flesh.

"Ah! I have it," soliloquized Aunt Sophronie; 'kins — kins — of our flesh and kins."

"Well," suggested Deluth, "do you think

the plural 'kins' quite correct or euphonious? and, coming after our flesh, is it not somewhat superlative, even in the singular?"

"I think you are quite right," sweetly responded Aunt Sophronie.

"I have it!" and her eyes rolled heavenward as she read the corrected stanza.

> "Each little twin,
> Tucked in a bin,
> Free from all sin,
> Is our beautiful kin.

"Ah, that's it, and in the singular, too, dear Mr. Deluth, as you suggested.

"What a grand thing is inspiration to the poet!

"Now, for the second verse."

"Oh, no," pleaded Deluth, quite alarmed. "You are not going to paralyze your brain with another verse!"

"Paralysis don't run in the Rodneys," exclaimed Aunt Sophronie; "and who ever heard of a poem in one poor little four-lined verse for twins? Now, then, the first line of verse second—This is it!" twirling her fingers again, and the poetess wrote:

"As they sleep in their crib——"

"Why, my dear Miss Rodney," interrupted Deluth, striving to look very serious, "in the first verse you put the twins asleep in their bin; now you are lifting them into a crib; that will never do."

Aunt Sophronie looked supremely wise, and elevating her chin, replied:

"It is quite evident you never tried your hand at poetry.

"Poetry is not law or selling dry goods, neither am I making out a brief or a dunning bill, therefore I must tell you concerning this, that lifting the children from a bin in the first verse to a crib in the second verse is poetic license, pure and simple."

Deluth closed his lips tightly, and looking intently at the shine on his boot toe, acquiesced.

"Ah! I knew you would see it in its proper light," she triumphantly replied.

"Which, the bin or the crib?"

"The poetry," and she played a tattoo with her pencil, evidently striving for inspiration to attack another line, while she slowly and quietly repeated—

> "As they sleep in their crib—
> Minus shoes, hat or bib."

"Isn't that simplicity itself?"

"Miss Rodney," exclaimed Deluth, as though awakening to the importance of this eventful birthday poem, "why not make them minus their hose and underclothing also?"

"Oh, dear!" drawled Aunt Sophronie, "if you were a poet you could understand that it is not at all necessary to mention the lack of one's entire garments to give an idea of nudity; or, in other words, stripped of everything save, for instance, their snow-white night-gowns—hold on! 'snow-white gown'; can't I get that in? it is beautifully poetic.

"Here it is!" touching her forehead with

the sweep of a great genius, and she proudly repeated—

> "As they sleep in their crib,
> Minus shoes, hat or bib,
> Rolled in snow-white night-gowns——"

"'Rolled,' repeated Deluth. "Why not have them *laid* in their gowns?"

"Why," she replied, instructively, "one can see '*rolled*' is much more poetic than simply 'laid' in their gowns. Anyone could say '*laid*,' but everyone would not think of '*rolled*.'

"Now the last line—don't move—

> "Rolled in snow-white night-gown,
> Pure and soft as swan's down——"

"Which are soft and pure?" asked Deluth, "the children, the gown or the down?"

"Why, the children, of course, are *pure*, and *soft* the gown and down.

"Just mentally transpose 'soft,' 'gown' and 'down,' and you will appreciate its sense eventually. You know we are obliged to *dwell* on modern poetry to fully enjoy its beauty. Let me read it all through.

"Each little twin,
Tucked in a bin,
Free from all sin,
Is our beautiful kin.

"As they sleep in their crib,
Minus hat, shoes or bib,
Rolled in snow-white night-gown,
Pure and soft as swan's down."

"It lacks finish—oh, yes, it does," as Deluth was about to interpose. "I have a very acute ear, keen perception and fullest appreciation, and I can see this lacks finish— Wait!" as she waived his objection with a grand flourish, and wrote—

"May the twins ever be
Fruit of old Rodney tree."

Deluth felt a convulsion which must soon betray him, but looking up suddenly saw a figure which gave him the longed for excuse to escape. "Pardon me, Miss Rodney, a friend," and he flew toward Victoria Lennox, who was just leaving a room adjoining.

CHAPTER V.

THE LAST WALTZ.

DELUTH hastily approached the object of his pursuit, who had just left the hostess, and exclaimed in a low voice, "Oh, Mrs. Lennox, I feared you would not come."

"Well," smilingly answered Victoria Lennox, "I am sure no one would have missed me. I only came because I promised Aunt Sophronie I would meet some members of a charity committee here, and so save an afternoon meeting, later."

"How can I thank you?" whispered Deluth, trembling with excitement.

"Why, Mr. Deluth," innocently replied Mrs. Lennox, "one would imagine my coming conferred on you some special honor."

"Honor," repeated Deluth, "is an empty word to express the pleasure your presence gives me."

"I do not understand you," said Mrs. Lennox, coldly, turning her eyes from him and preparing to leave his side.

"No, certainly you do not," answered Deluth. "I fail to understand myself. The next number is a waltz, may I have the pleasure?"

"I have decided," unconcernedly replied Victoria, "never to waltz again."

"Ah," gasped Deluth, as though a knife had pierced his heart. "Do not say that! For weeks I have lived on the anticipation of waltzing with you to-night."

"How very remarkable, not to say foolish," lightly returned Victoria, wishing to leave him.

"Foolish," repeated Deluth, "to those who cannot appreciate that sentiment which has absorbed me since first I met you."

"Mr. Deluth, you forget yourself," indignantly rejoined Victoria. "Mr. Lennox would scarcely relish such remarks to his wife. I must decline to further listen to your folly," and Victoria reached for her fan, which he held.

Deluth was baffled, but not discouraged.

His knowledge of human nature told him Victoria Lennox was far beyond the shallow women he had flattered, won, and as quickly tossed aside for new conquests. He rapidly solved his next move, as he thought, "I will appeal to her pity—the strongest weakness of a good woman."

Victoria, noticing Deluth's bowed head, little imagined his devilish thoughts, and judging she had spoken harshly, innocently remarked: "Mr. Deluth, you must pardon me if I have wounded you. I—I—really did not mean, but you know you should not speak to your friend's wife as you have just spoken to me. However, you meant no harm, I am sure. We will forget it has occurred."

Deluth here gave a sigh of relief, which to unsophisticated Victoria sounded like suddenly opened flood-gates of deepest grief.

"Oh, Mrs. Lennox!" exclaimed he, "how can I apologize for the foolish betrayal of myself. After to-night I promise never again to intrude my feelings upon you, no matter how I suffer."

Victoria's honest brown eyes now looked at this demon with as much pity as though her words had consigned him to the executioner. Seeing the effect he had produced, Deluth followed up his vantage.

"I have but one last favor to ask of you," said he.

Believing his "favor" was not to "expose his conversation to her husband," and feeling that course would only cause needless trouble, Victoria quickly replied, "Oh! I will grant anything I can, certainly, with pleasure."

"It is," rejoined he, "for one waltz——"

"No, no, not that!" impulsively burst from Victoria.

"You promised," pointedly added Deluth, "anything; you will keep your word. Your husband is not here to forbid you."

"Mr. Lennox has not forbidden me," defiantly responded Victoria; "but he does not waltz and I believe does not like me to waltz."

"Oh," sneered Deluth, wholly off his guard, "he is another of the jealous husbands who never wish a wife to have any pleasure which is not centered in themselves."

"That is not true of Mr. Lennox," indignantly replied Victoria. "He is kindness and goodness itself, and contributes in every way possible to my happiness. I do not fear my husband, but it is my greatest pleasure to respect his very reasonable wishes."

"Will you give me this waltz?" insisted Deluth.

Victoria hesitated, tapped her slipper nervously, looked at Deluth, whom she saw would hold her to her promise, then answered coldly and with measured precision, "Simply to keep my word, then, since you demand it, but that shall be my last. I shall never waltz again."

Ah, how much misery would be spared, did the erring heed the voice of conscience, which silently protests against that fateful "only once more!"

Mrs. Lennox expected that her husband, who had been absent some weeks, might arrive shortly after midnight, therefore had only gone to the reception to meet the committee, according to her aunt Sophronie's request. She had not, in consequence, removed an extra wrap, being anxious to get home to welcome Jack Lennox, who was worthy of all the love of his fond wife. She now accepted Deluth's arm and was escorted to the ladies' dressing room, where she left him to eagerly await her return.

No sooner was Victoria rid of Deluth's presence than she became terrified with herself.

"I am going to waltz again with that man, he, who from the first time his arms encircled me in that familiar dance, has exercised the most fearful spell over me. Thank heaven! he does not suspect it.

"How I loathe him! Why did I not rudely leave him? Well, it is only to redeem my word. I shall *never* waltz again!"

This good resolve drove away all sadness from her face, and when she reappeared Deluth thought she had never looked so beautiful.

Although Victoria was grace itself, she

had danced but little, and a few turns of the waltz left her helplessly dizzy in the arms of the unscrupulous Deluth.

Closer he drew her to him. Closer he pressed her to his throbbing breast. Closer he bent his face to hers, until in a burst of passionate eloquence he poured forth a story of undying love.

Victoria was in an enchanted dream. The music, the flowers, the beautiful figures gliding around her had intoxicated this pure woman, whose only remaining senses told her she was floating in air, and no longer of the earth earthy.

On, on they went in the maddening waltz, the devil still sending forth his poisonous whispers.

On, on they went, his hot breath burning his dastardly appeals for sympathy into her very brain.

She could now no longer hear anything but the seductive music, and with her blinded vision could only think, "I am floating in air—floating in air—in air."

CHAPTER VI.

THE HUSBAND'S RETURN.

JACK LENNOX had reached the depot wild with delight that he was so near home and in a few moments more would clasp in his arms the woman whom he loved with the strongest feelings of his great and noble nature.

It was near midnight. He had not telegraphed his expected arrival, preferring to steal in upon his idol, encircle her in his arms and smother her with love-kisses before she discovered the intruder of her chamber.

"Drive quickly," and he handed the cabman twice his fare to speed him to his home.

The lights in his house were turned low, and as he inserted his night-key cautiously, he smiled like a boy planning a great surprise. Silently he closed the doors, and cautiously mounted the stairway; breathlessly he entered his wife's sleeping apartments, until his ecstatic lips touched her very pillow.

"Not here!" he gasped. Hastily he shot up the light, fiercely he rang a bell, and quickly learned where Mrs. Lennox had gone, with the additional comforting information that she had told her maid she would remain but a short time.

"Ah, then she thought I might come tonight," soliloquized the relieved husband, and quickly donning an evening suit, departed for the Asvanderlets'.

A few words with the hostess, who added much to his pleasure by remarking: "Mrs. Lennox told me she would remain but a few moments, as she would not for worlds be absent when you might arrive home. There is devotion for you."

Jack Lennox speedily singled out his beautiful wife, but his happiness was somewhat dimmed when he saw her waltzing, and with Deluth.

"Oh," sighed the momentarily unhappy husband, "why have I never requested Victoria to desist from that immodest dance? To stand here and see my loved one hugged to the breast of another man, even though he were not the worst of *roués*, is horrifying. I will tell her my feelings to-night concerning this hugging to music, and I know she will forever spare me another such painful sight."

Satisfied with this decision, and seeing Mrs. Lennox approaching, he stepped into the dimly-lighted conservatory and slipped behind a portiere, still bent on giving Victoria a little surprise.

A moment more, instead of passing, she entered the conservatory on the arm of Deluth, who, still pouring forth the poison, was saying:

"And you cannot deny that my influence over you is the same. I read it in your liquid eyes, I feel it in your quivering body, I know it in your unconscious creeping to my breast, your throbbing heart beating against my own. Deny it! Deny it if you can, while I imprint my love!"

Until now the dreamy, waltz-intoxicated

woman was speechless, but the profane touch of that demon's lips instantly recalled her scattered senses.

Like a tigress she sprang back from him, but too late. A grasp on the curtain at her side relaxed, and Jack Lennox fell senseless at the feet of his terrified wife.

CHAPTER VII.

A THIRD VICTIM.

EUNICE PENDERS, a bride of two winters, appeared at the Rodney home.

"Why, Eunice, I am so glad to see you," said Mrs. Rodney. "We missed you from church two Sabbaths, and fearing you were ill, I was about to run over. Mr. Penders is well, I trust."

Mrs. Penders felt as if her heart was in her throat, and as she attempted to reply, an avalanche of tears answered for her.

"Why, my dear, what is it? do tell me," sympathetically entreated Mrs. Rodney, as she drew near her friend.

Mrs. Penders strove to resist sobbing, and tremblingly asked:

"You haven't heard?"

Mrs. Rodney, thoroughly alarmed, replied:

"I have heard nothing."

"'Well,' hesitatingly began Mrs. Penders, "it was the night of the orphans' ball. Mr. Penders is very fond of dancing, or rather waltzing, in fact he never does any but the round dances. He was waltzing with Mrs. Hayes, when suddenly Mr. Hayes stood by me, looking very much excited. As Mr. Penders came up to seat Mrs. Hayes, her husband said to her:

"'I forbade you to waltz again with that man!' pointing to Mr. Penders, who, as excitedly, inquired the meaning of such public insult.

"Mr. Hayes replied:

"'You may call it *public insult*, since your frequent waltzing this entire season with my wife, from being privately commented upon, is now publicly spoken of.

"'Mrs. Hayes has been told of this also. I first requested her to silence gossip by declining to appear again with you, and she refused.

"'She now defies me; therefore, I warn both of you: if this is repeated she must seek protection elsewhere than from the man whom her justly-censured conduct dishonors!'

"At this Mrs. Hayes told her husband that she would waltz with Mr. Penders wherever and whenever he asked her, despite all the gossipings in the universe.

"'Then,' said Mr. Penders to Mrs. Hayes, 'you have my protection at any time Mr. Hayes sees fit to withdraw his.'

"Mr. Hayes was about to strike Tom, when I quickly stepped between them, and told Mrs. Hayes that I, also, objected to such inseparable companionship as they had evinced, and declined emphatically to consent to any further monopoly of Mr. Penders.

"The result of it all was, Mr. Penders left town the next day, and Mrs. Hayes the day after. No one seems to know anything of either of them."

"Oh, that waltzing again! wretched woman and wretched man, though he is your husband."

"Husband!" scornfully repeated Mrs. Penders; "he is my husband no longer!" and burst into tears.

"By-bye, mamma," said the twins, Roby and Ruby, as they ran in and held up their pink lips to be kissed by their mother, who gave this parting injunction to Roby:

"Darling, you will meet your playfellow, Jimmie Vaintone, whom you struck when you last played with him. You never will commit such a shocking act again."

Roby's eyes flashed as he replied :

"Yeth, he will 'member to haave hissef, too, and not call sister twomboy ag'in."

"Yeth, he did, mamma," said Ruby, "and brover just struck him good. Ha! ha! ha!" and both children laughed at the recollection of Roby's resolute courage.

"My daughter," exclaimed Mrs. Rodney, "I am shocked at you. Do you not know it is dreadful for little boys and girls to quarrel? Nurse must inform me if you do anything naughty at play this afternoon, and if so, you shall not visit again in a long time."

"Oh, we'll be dood, mamma," spoke up Ruby for herself and brother, as Roby, with his little pursed-up mouth and erect head, seemed rather doubtful about never striking a boy again.

The twins for the first time noticed "Auntie Penders," as they called her, whose eyes, they saw, were red with weeping. They gazed at her in wonderment, until Ruby cautiously approached her and softly volunteered the information, "Aunty Penders, did you know you was cwyin'?"

Before Eunice could reply between her smiles and tears, Roby strode up and majestically demanded:

"Auntie, you tell me who made you cwy, and I'll lick him so him never make you cwy ag'in."

The childish sympathy relieved Mrs. Penders, who smilingly consoled the little ones.

"Now, run along, dears. Nurse, return in two hours," said Mrs. Rodney, while sweet little voices echoed:

"Mamma, by-bye," and they were gone to play with eight or ten others, including the aforesaid belabored Jim.

Mr. Rodney, who had just arrived, peeped in.

"I thought I heard voices," said he. "Mrs. Penders, I hope you are quite well."

As Mrs. Penders replied she stole a look at his face, which told her he knew all.

"I see you have heard of Mr. Penders," said she.

"Yes!" indignantly answered Mr. Rodney; "I learned of it to-day. I cannot understand my friend Tom's disgraceful conduct. He was apparently so devoted. We have often remarked how happy you always seemed together. How did this occur? How did it begin?"

"By waltzing with Mrs. Hayes," flashed Mrs. Penders.

"And Mrs. Hayes waltzing with Mr. Penders," said Mr. Rodney. "Nothing very remarkable about that, except that this is the third waltzing scandal which has come to light of late; how many victims not known, we can imagine. This waltzing, I believe, is responsible for a big ratio of misery in polite society."

"I never knew Tom so wild for dancing as in the past year," remarked Mrs. Penders.

"Twice he left a sick-bed to attend parties, where he did every round dance—and with Sibyl Hayes."

"Why did you permit it?" inquired Mrs. Rodney.

"What could I do?" helplessly asked Mrs. Penders.

"Do!" said Nell Rodney, her eyes flashing. "My husband would cease such public offense to me, or I would place myself on the defensive."

"Bravo! my dear," applauded Mr. Rodney; "but failing to recall such a husband to his natural senses, what then?"

"Yes, what then?" seconded Mrs. Penders, who saw that Mrs. Rodney had reached the brink of argument.

"What, then?" repeated Mrs. Rodney. "Well, if I could not touch his pride, I would at least establish the fact that he could not wound my feelings without proper resentment."

"Ah, my dear," said Eunice Penders, "it is so easy to suggest what others should do; but once become the victim, you would see things somewhat different than as a spectator."

"Well, I would do something," replied Mrs. Rodney, emphatically, as though that mysterious "something" was the most fearful punishment ever meted out to unfortunate humanity. "And now you are striving to break your heart over that wretch—I see it.

"Just go home, get a few things you will need—your servants can look after the house—and you remain here until that miscreant comes to his senses. No, no! You shall not remain alone while we can make your misery a little lighter by sharing it with you!

"My dear, every house has its skeleton, which will sometime stalk forth. But the wary lock it tightly in, so that listeners can only occasionally hear the rattling of its telltale bones. Return in twenty minutes; no more crying;" and kissing her affectionately, she literally bundled her off and watched Mr. Rodney close her in the *coupé*.

"My dear," observed Mr. Rodney, "you

have done a great kindness to Mrs. Penders in asking her here; and after noting your magnificent Susan-B.-Anthony spirit just now, I believe within the next twelve-month you will be offered the presidency of the 'Sorosis,' or the first woman's-rights club in New York. Ha! ha! What costume will you adopt?"

"Ned, dear, if ever I should have so proud a distinction conferred on me, I do not think I should seek to improve on woman's present simple, graceful garment.

"At all events, I would be too deeply engrossed by striving to correct abuses engendered and overlooked by you wonderful 'lords of creation.'"

"Speaking of costumes," remarked Aunt Sophronie, who had just entered, "in the Bishop's comparison, Centennial Day, to the 'Washingtonian manners, which,' as he said, 'we have banished,' don't you think he intended to include ceremonious dress, also?"

"I could not say," replied Mrs. Rodney; "perhaps I am unduly sensitive in the matter, for I fear the most eloquent sermon would fail to impress me, if a clergyman stood in the pulpit outlined in inexcusable dress. I sometimes see persons of intelligence so inappropriately clothed that it starts the perspiration of disappointment oozing down my back like threads of unfeeling icicles.

"Form and ceremony, certainly, in its proper place, is essential to a polite people. Those who seek to dispense with it are not of the most cultured. With God's great rule and order, He also teaches proper adornment; otherwise, why, after providing the necessaries of life, did He shower upon us the beautiful in nature?

"He has surrounded us with richest specimens. Just think of twelve hundred varieties of the lily alone; and out of the two hundred thousand species of insects, see the exquisite coloring and care the Divine Being has bestowed on a tiny beetle's wing.

"Not a rock, plant, wave of sea or fleecy cloud has He overlooked, from the gorgeous-hued tropic to the aurora of the arctic; from the coral abyss of the ocean to the grandly towering snow-capped mountain.

"The blossom which lives but for a night is painted as exquisitely as if never to wither and die. The lightest vapor is as perfect as though not to sail away and disappear, even while we gaze in admiration at its spirituelle loveliness.

"And with nature's constant rehabilitating, does not each successive dressing, in a cultivated garden, come out more perfect than before?

"Can intelligence deny that all this is sent for our imitation, and to inspire us with a love of our Creator's grand, symmetrical, exquisite, delicate, enchanting, surpassingly beautiful workmanship, until its proper appreciation tends to ennoble and bring us nearer to our God?"

After a moment's silence Aunt Sophronie straightened herself and ejaculated:

"I'd like to know what buffoon introduced a gentleman's evening dress for waiters.

"I am always so annoyed when I see it, Nell, that if you will permit me, at your next reception, I will robe every female servant in the house just like yourself—and while you are doing social honors, see if they look appropriately dressed for their respective duties; then, perhaps, we could appreciate the absurdity of the 'waiter costume.'

"Any wonder so many servants' heads get turned striving to ape their masters' and mistresses' dressing, in form, color and extravagance?"

"Pitch in, Aunt; vote against it," said Mr. Rodney, encouragingly. "Why, I did not think it was so late. An office full of clients by this time;" and kissing his wife, while not forgetting his idolizing aunt, he stepped out with that smiling, light heart, so unmistakable in the contented and happy husband.

About this time the children had exhausted nearly every other sport, when Roby was elected captain, to head a company of soldiers.

"Ip! I is goin' to be cap'in; the mens must be sojers, marching wif their wifs," said Roby.

"Dere ain't womens 'nuff," suggested little Vera Marshall, "for every mans to has a wife."

"No, there ain't," acquiesced Florence Browning.

Ruby proceeded to count, "One, two, free, four, fibe, tix, seben mens; one, two, free womens—dats all."

After serious consideration Captain Roby announced:

"One mens must be a womans; den it will be jus' wight."

Turning to Johnnie Goodall, who was a sort of lieutenant plenipotentiary, he commissioned him to "git a boy to be a womans."

Johnnie proceeded to question the other five, beginning with Willie Rice.

"You, Willie Withe, be the other womans?"

"Naw," drawled Willie, looking the picture of disgust.

"Henny Drew, will you be the other womans?"

"Naw, thir!" savagely answered Henry.

"Kirkie Loomith, will you be the——"

"You nee'n' asthk me; I won't be no womans," interrupted Kirkie.

"Naw me—naw me!" quickly chimed in little Walter Blakely, knowing his turn would come next.

Now thoroughly discouraged, Johnnie waxed desperate, and made a final attack on the most and always disobliging of the boys.

"Jim Vaintone, you got to be the other womans."

"Naw, I won't," said Jim, sulkily.

"Well," said Johnnie, who was beginning to lose all patience, "Willie won't be 'er, Henny won't be 'er, Kirkie won't be 'er, and Walter won't be 'er. You ith the latht one; you *got* to be 'er, so we can have our p'rade."

"I wouldn't be no womans, cos my pa says he hates womans; cos womans is mean—guess he knows."

At this interesting juncture Roby came up and informed Jim thuswise:

"My mamma ith a womans—her ain't

mean; sister ith a womans—her ain't mean, ith her ?"

"Yas, she is," drawled Jim, while his nose looked as though sniffing an unpleasant odor, at which Roby's forbearance gave way, and the next moment found Jim, amidst tears and imprecations, sprawling on the ground.

"Now, Roby Wodney, you'll see when I tell your ma."

"I tole youm mover," said Roby, defiantly, "that I wouldn't strucked you leth you 'bused sister. Youm did 'buse sister, callin' her mean, so I strucked you ag'in. I gueth you will 'haave youmthelf now."

"Sojers, take youm wifs," and as the boys quickly fell in line with their 'wives' Roby played a toodle de toot on an improvised cornet made from a fire shovel, and marched his men as valiantly around the garden as though equipped with fife and drum and every implement of deadliest battle-field.

CHAPTER VIII.

FIRE AT SEA.

THE steamers Cullard and Inman, racing in mid-ocean in January, was a pleasant surprise to all the passengers except Victoria Lennox, who did not leave her stateroom until the Inman dropped behind at nightfall. Robed in a disguise which fully accorded with her hopeless sadness, a widow's outfit of deepest mourning, she then ascended the upper deck.

As she looked into the dark waters she exclaimed, "Not to-night; I have not the courage." She turned quickly and selected a sequestered seat. Although wrapped in fur, the piercing breeze passed through her delicate body as if she were dressed in phantom gauze.

But she heeded not, her thoughts were no longer of herself, but of her beloved husband left far, far behind, with a broken heart as his only companion.

"My love," she cried, "I was mad, not guilty. Save me! Save me before it is too late." But love's wings could not span the billowy distance to rescue her. She gazed across the receding waters in pathetic entreaty. "See, how I am borne from you! Reach forth your loving arms and bring me home to peace and love.

"O God! Reverse thy wheels of time! turn back my life one week!"

But the rushing of the ponderous steamer mockingly echoed her mental moanings:

"Bearing me away! further away!! forever away!!!"

The bells of the ship had just struck eight, and "All's well" greeted the listeners' ears. The night was blackest darkness. Sharp winds played the most doleful *misereres*. Everything seemed weird, strange, ghastly.

What a change from that of one week before for the beloved and honored Mrs. Lennox; she bowed her head in an agony of grief and sobbed aloud.

Suddenly a gentle voice recalled her.

"Madam, can I do anything for you?"

Victoria was startled into raising her beautiful face for one moment, then quickly turned her head as she recognized a young clergyman who had led the Sabbath service.

Mrs. Lennox replied in a quiet way that she was not ill, only a "little homesick," and apologized for disturbing anyone, adding that she thought herself "quite alone."

Her beautiful eyes had already won the rector's admiration, but when the sweet voice gave utterance, Cupid's darts penetrated his heart.

"I trust you will pardon my foolishness," said Victoria. "I am hysterical sometimes, and to-night I seem to completely give way to sad thoughts, which make me, oh! so homesick." Her quivering lips could say no more, and again she burst into convulsive sobbings.

The rector's eyes grew moist, in sympathy, and seating himself beside her he strove to soothe her sorrow.

"Homesickness," said he, "was the first

grief of my young life. When eight years of age I was visiting relatives only a few blocks distant; about midnight I awakened with that deathlike feeling, homesickness. Bribery of the most fascinating description was resorted to, but every effort to pacify me was futile. I still begged for home, to which I was finally taken; when my tears ceased, and I was again happy with my parents.

"My child," and he looked at the deep mourning of widowhood. "You are homesick with longings for those you have lost in this world, but strive to think of our heavenly Parent, who will shortly take you to that everlasting home where you will be reunited with your loved ones.

"What a comfort to know that after all our sorrows here such a home awaits us, where we will have no more separations, no more homesickness, and where we will know no more sorrow. Think of it, my child. Commune with your heavenly Father, and he will lighten your burdened heart."

Victoria wiped her streaming eyes, and arose with a sense of peace she could not understand. She quietly thanked the rector, who opened the door of the companion-way. As she passed in she heard dancing music, and looking down observed a number of people trying to waltz. The sight, which too vividly recalled one week before, made her reel back to the deck, as she exclaimed, "That deadly waltz!"

The rector caught the words and answered her.

"I am glad to know that you abhor that immodest dance. Think of wives, mothers and daughters being embraced by a variety of men, sometimes utter strangers, with 'music' as the only excuse for such monstrous familiarity. The clergy can trace the misery of fashionable people more to the demoralizing practice of waltzing than to any other cause. Yet the fashionable world seeks to shroud the immorality of this danger, which destroys so many homes and wrecks so many lives. If estranged friends and the divorce courts chose to tell the beginning of the end, an appalling number could be traced to this curse of the modern ball-room, the hugging to music waltz."

"Ah," sighed Victoria, as she thought, "to that curse I owe my misery." Every word of the rector was like a lancet driven into her heart. She longed to lay bare her grief and beg for sympathy, but she dared not, something held her back, till she could only think and tremble.

The rector continued: "In a certain foreign society, and in remote apings of other countries, including our own, to permit an unmarried daughter to walk to church with a gentleman, or formally receive him under the protective canopy of her parents' roof, which we are wont to feel breathes the benedictory atmosphere of sacred home, would be something shocking, if unattended by a chaperone; yet this extreme surveillance of a properly brought up girl bounds to such an inconsistent, astoundingly familiar antithesis, with *ma fille*, at a ball, thrown straight into the arms of the first social *roués* who think worth while to check off a waltzing number from her programme, and thus carve and serve up feminine modesty in a tenth, twentieth vulgar embrace; all decorously swallowed in ball-room flavoring, garnished only with symphony notes to excuse this disgraceful custom, hugging to music.

"With members of my church, I both enjoy and encourage music, the drama, and all innocent, health-giving amusements. I am also pleased to witness the dancing of respectable, graceful, beautiful measures, and delight in a rollicking reel and jig of the pure-minded peasant; but against the immodest, vulgar, promiscuous hugging to music, I raise my voice in condemnation, and knowingly, I will not administer the sacrament to a communicant of my church who indulges in the habit of such appallingly indecent conduct."

"Ah," exclaimed Victoria, "if all clergymen took that stand, how much misery would be saved the innocent! There is one life dear to me which would not now be forever blighted."

"The waltz," replied the rector, "is like the candle which lures the unsuspicious insect to its fascinating light, unconscious that it nears the fire, until its wings are scorched and the death-heat penetrates its vitals."

"God prosper you," said Victoria. "Your labor will not be in vain. Good-night," and Mrs. Lennox again turned to reach her state-room. As Dr. Wadsworth took her hand to steady her, the ship gave a tremendous lurch, which hurled Victoria into the very arms of the rector.

Then came a terrific explosion as of a thousand cannon. In a moment the heavens seemed ablaze. A volume of fire shot forth like the bursting of a veritable hell. Voices arose in the most terrifying shrieks of "Fire! fire!! fire!!!"

Before Victoria or the rector could recover their equipoise, men, women and children had flocked to the deck. The cries increased until the demoniac shrieks of the crew and the heartrending moanings of the passengers made the awful scene a pandemonium of the bottomless pit.

"Lower the boats! Lower the boats!" shouted and roared the captain.

Just then the racing steamer hove in sight.

"The Inman, thank God!" went up from every tongue. With savage greed the crimson flames licked the deck, eager for its prey as the hungry tiger lapping the blood of its expiring victim.

The rector had dragged Victoria to where the women and children were already being lowered into boats, but once there, Mrs. Lennox refused to stir until the mothers and helpless little ones had been let down.

"Fur God's sake let me pass!" cried an appealing voice at Victoria's side. "Let me pass with my boy! A million dollars fur a boat to save my boy!"

As though all instinctively felt the presence of death, even midst the terrible excitement, a way was cleared for the frantic father, and a moment later Joe Jungle sprang down the ladder and into the lifeboat carrying the lifeless form of litt'e Hank.

The Wayback could not realize that the dark messenger had claimed his idol, and from the moment he was taken aboard wildly strove to revive the inanimate remains.

"Hank! Hank! it's Pop! On'y look at me jess once, Hank! We're all right neow, percious boy! Look at Pop! Look at Pop! Ye needn't be frightened neow! Thar' ain't no fire here, Hank! Oh, Hank, look at Pop! See the stars, Hank! The big moon's shinin' tew! It's snowin', Hank! Come on, we'll git yer sled, an' here's yer dog waitin' ter draw ye. Open yer eyes an' see it's all right. Look at Pop! Look at Pop, Hank! Why you're cold, Hank! You're cold! You're sti—— My God! he's dead!"

The Wayback's voice sounded like the plaintive moan of a mother suddenly robbed of her child.

Infidelity was forgotten in Joe Jungle's appealing wail, "O God! God! Give me back my boy!"

CHAPTER IX.

SAVED.

NEARLY every woman and child had been safely placed in boats, when, as Victoria turned, she came upon Dr. Wadsworth, who was supporting the burned and almost senseless form of Lord Oakdale.

"I cannot wait," said the rector to Mrs. Lennox. "Tell the men to take him next," but away the rector darted, seemingly into the very flames.

Lord Oakdale, the son and petted heir to a dukedom, who had been reared in luxury, whose slightest wishes had always seemed commands to be obeyed, even by his equals; but who, to the casual observer, was inane to a degree, had suddenly evinced a bravery composed of rarest metal.

A few moments before he had listened in amusement to the sneers and intentional insults of Joe Jungle, and had then crushed through the fiery flames to save the Wayback's idolized child, at the almost certain loss of his own life.

But heroism such as his never stops to count the cost; like the soldier on the battle-field he knows not cowardice, and fear to him is as great a stranger as a tropical sun to the arctic regions.

He now lay perfectly helpless, and was suffering the most excruciating agony, but human power could do nothing for him there, and it was doubtful if his life could be saved even under the most favorable circumstances.

"Carry him down the ladder for the next boat," cried Victoria, who was supporting Lord Oakdale's head; but the ugliest phase of human nature, which is termed self-preservation, but usually means cowardly selfishness, seemed to possess every creature to whom she appealed.

She might as well have expected raving cattle, under a shower of fire, to heed her words.

"Oh, men of strength, will you leave a hero-brother here to burn? Have you no hearts?"

But no one came to her. The rector was still assisting some elderly people and fainting invalids, who would not otherwise have been saved.

When Victoria looked at Lord Oakdale, whose sacrifice of self had brought him so near death, and thought that he must lie there, food for the devouring flames, she became almost insane. She sprang to her feet and cried:

"Fathers!" and her voice rose above the hiss of the flames—mounted above moans—echoed beyond shrieks. "Are there no fathers here, grateful to a fellow-being who has nearly given his life to save a little child? Will no grateful father carry this dying man to the life-boat?"

In a moment Mrs. Lennox was surrounded by strong men, who in a twinkling had raised the now senseless burden, whose flesh was literally falling from his hands, and bore him down the ladder to the transfer boat.

Brave Lord Oakdale! Stout heart! You prove we are not all animal, for God the Infinite shines through the finite in such sacrifice.

Victoria had seen the last fainting woman passed over, when a terrible resolve she had already made took form.

"No further will I go, Charles Deluth!" thought she. "While I am still innocent I will seek death before living under the stigma of shame you have purposely cast over me."

As she was being put forward for the next boat, she slipped by the men. With a prayer on her lips for forgiveness, she commended her soul to her Maker and sprang into the sea.

A sailor, who had witnessed her bravery in assisting the frantic women and children, saw her mad leap, and shouted, "Woman overboard!"

No one heeded even this startling information, at such a perilous moment, but the rector quickly ran to where Victoria had stood a moment before. She was gone!

Nearer and nearer came the flames, the devouring demon now hissing its forked tongue into the very faces of those left on deck, but Dr. Wadsworth cared not to save himself; in an instant he had torn off his outer coat and plunged into the watery deep.

Victoria's body had risen for the second time when the rector caught her in his arms, which, though naturally powerful, were weakened by the terrible exertion and excitement on the ship.

He now attempted to swim toward the Inman, but his strength was so far gone he could make but little headway. His weak voice could not be heard above the shriekings of men and women, and he at last felt he must resign himself to death.

He could no longer see. The last flickering rays of intelligence were fading away, but he clung all the more determinedly to his precious burden. Just then he felt something strike his arm, which recalled his senses sufficiently to hear a voice, "Catch the rope! Catch the rope!" Mechanically he caught it, was quickly dragged to a lifeboat, and insensibly transferred, with his priceless treasure, to the Inman.

The rector soon rallied and assisted the surgeons who were striving to revive Mrs. Lennox. After half an hour of untiring labor they ceased, and muttered, "No use, she's gone!" But Dr. Wadsworth still labored over the seemingly lifeless remains. After awhile a feeble pulsation was noticeable, Victoria's lips moved, her eyes opened, she was saved!

"She lives, thank heaven! she lives!" gasped the rector, whose devotion and crowning success brought tears to the eyes of every one present.

Charles Deluth had managed, by assisting children, to get into the first boat, and was thus transferred to the haven of safety; the strongest trait in his type of character—cowardice—evincing itself at the first sign of danger. He now walked around, nervously peering into rooms, sheepishly looking among groups. As he came upon one he started back like a criminal, when he saw the woman who was the object of attention.

"Ah," said one of the onlookers, who had noticed Deluth's dastardly conduct, "your friend, the beautiful widow, was nearly gone; fell overboard, faint with fatigue by trying to save the helpless, while you were in the first boat, taking such good care of your mustache."

Deluth, believing he had escaped unobserved, was stunned, but summoning all his habitual effrontery, stepped to Victoria's side, and with a show of great anxiety, whispered: "You are safe! When I missed you I thought you had been taken in the first boat."

Victoria closed her eyes to shut out the hateful vision. The surgeon called, "Stand back!" while he tenderly took Mrs. Lennox in his arms and conveyed her to the captain's room, in which the kind-hearted commander had given orders to place her.

Recording angels of "noblest heroism" transcribed the supernal bravery of Royal Wadsworth.

CHAPTER X.

NO NEWS.

MRS. PENDERS was seated by the window in the Rodney library. The threatening sky was shooting forth its angry darts, while the rolling heavens seemed ready to be dashed to earth by demon hands—fit accompaniment to her turbulent thoughts. As she sat with folded arms and veiled eyes, living over the sorrowful past, which had worse than widowed the once adoring wife, a crash of thunder made her start and shudder.

Just then her mail was handed her, over which she hurriedly glanced.

"Another day passed and no news from him," she murmured in dejection. "Why did I ever marry him—a fickle, brainless creature, who has sacrificed me through a contemptible dance?

"I am beginning to hate him more than I ever loved him. I will never look upon his face again, and were he to fall on his knees before me I would not forgive him."

Mr. and Mrs. Rodney now entered, chatting upon events of the morning. Finally the former took up the papers for a cursory perusal.

"Hear us question England, 'Why don't you give up the little kingdom which has grown tired of your dictation, and wishes to rule herself? Your stubbornness is unparalleled.'

"To be sure, we are a recently steeped-in-blood family, who coolly butchered each other for an identical principle—secession; but then Americans could have no such nonsense as that *here*, you know. When we, a Republic, would not permit a sister State to secede, what laughable inconsistency to expect the most powerful monarchy to release one of her children!

"If the naturally quick, brilliant Irish labored in their own country one-tenth they are forced to in America, for the barest competency; devoted their energies to opening gold-repaying industries, instead of being longer fooled into supporting absorbing societies, they could restore beautiful Ireland, regain business patronage and respect, and command the admiration of the world.

"When a class began to languish in indolence, complaint naturally followed against the landlord who dared expect any returns from his property, even sufficient to pay his taxes, and this, in many cases, after years and years of indulgent waiting. There are exceptions to all generalities, but in the main the landlords of Ireland, anterior to the assassination era, were the most lenient in the civilized world. Their very mistaken kindness in postponing the collection of their dues gradually taught inactivity to the peasantry and dulled their ambition against laboring for anything beyond the merest subsistence, until their wildly simple lives became a pastoral of easy existence, as they provided for themselves only the plainest necessities and those which required the least possible exertion. It is when they forsake their pastoral ease for the American continent, their eyes are opened."

"Yes," smiled Mrs. Rodney, "as in the case of our cook's cousin. Some time after Pat's arrival his friends found him a very reasonable boarding place, and mentioned the price. In indignant astonishment Pat asked, 'An' would they be chargin' in Amerikay for a bed, an' the bit a man ates? An' me workin' like a horse, as I niver worked in Ireland?'

"Innocent Pat has found that everyone must pay his way in America, and labor here means more than lying on a velvety greensward, talking to the sparrows.

"Pat may be more surprised to learn that if men, women or children are found begging in our streets for a crust of bread, they are arrested and imprisoned; still, our government, to its shame be it said, supplies no labor for the suffering honest, whereby they may earn bare food and heat, even during our fearful winters.

"State labor, which should be ever ready for emergencies to the willing workman, is by our government turned over to prison labor contractors, whereas criminals could be colonized on some of our immense tracts of vacant, beautiful country, and so given opportunity to recommence lives which here, in the midst of their evil association and temptation, are worthless.

"Released from prisons to sin anew, then back to their familiar death-chains, working to swell the purse of speculators, and thus robbing honest labor of its unquestionable right. Yet we wish to be known as a 'superior nation.'

"The destitute who would gladly labor, in preference to accepting compulsory charity, sometimes fall senseless, from cold or hunger, before the red-tape of our charity commissions respond to their dire need; no more common sense or humanity being displayed toward them than though they appealed for blue collars or purple fans, instead of sustaining food and sufficient warmth wherewith to drive from themselves and loved ones the blackest of death's messengers.

"Were it not for our big-hearted people of wealth, who so generously provide homes, private hospitals and constant personal relief, God help the suffering poor, for our laws of charity are rendered, by some who so indolently and others who so infamously execute them, totally inadequate to meet urgent immediate necessities.

"By three days' notice, a heartless landlord, for a few days' overdue rent, may drive forth tenants, men, women and children, actually dying of hunger and disease, and put them on the street, in any weather, which brotherly kindness is performed every day in New York. Yet no delinquent tenant is expected to relegate the landlord to that bourne from which no rent-gatherer returns; and the landlords justify their acts by saying, 'It is the *law* that we may *evict* for *non-payment* of our *dues* after *three days*.'

"The Northern Pacific Railroad, a short time since, evicted, within one week, over four hundred settlers and their families, as the commissioners of the Land Office decided that the land belonged to the railroad belt. The ejected, in many cases, were left without means of subsistence. So suddenly and cruelly were these evictions made, that the city authorities of Brainard, Minnesota, were compelled to telegraph for aid to prevent starvation, yet no one seized a shotgun with which to ventilate the domes of the railroad agents.

"The railroad officials say it is lawful to take possession of their own property, and that the building of railroads opens new countries, extends civilization, and benefits millions, not only in commercial advantages, but by furnishing employment to hundreds of thousands.

"But had such a case, with minor ones of daily occurrence, taken place under a monarchical government, the civilized world would have been startled with tales of cruelty unparalleled, and we would have been the first to call public meetings to protest against such legalized 'man's inhumanity to man.'

"Strange how a cable announcement to

us magnifies some legal transaction of another country into a diabolical horror at the very moment we are unconcernedly justifying its counterpart, or worse, at home. A number of Americans had grown to terming 'anarchy' 'struggles for liberty,' until we had a little taste of the 'struggle' at a base (bomb) ball rehearsal, which draped seven homes in mourning and enlightened our benighted understanding to the fact that anarchists were not loving supporters of a free Republic, unless the 'freedom' permitted them to murder those who disagreed with their superior (?) ideas, whereupon the assassinating 'pitchers' were taken by twelve catchers and legally transferred to the 'shortstop,' 'Law.'

"This quelled the bloodthirsty for a short time, but they are hot planning matches again, and in this civilized land and metropolis held a public meeting in a hall to rejoice on the ninth anniversary of the assassination of the Czar. They applauded his murderers and cracked jokes over his sudden taking off; made speeches in commendation of those who had sworn, or would swear, to send the present ruler to join his father before another twelvemonth; enthused the desperadoes in the audience, until they howled with delight, and expressed their eagerness to sniff the blood of the proposed victim, or of anyone who thwarted their diabolical plans.

"We have a law—occasionally obsolete—clearly defining public speeches '*which incite to riot and bloodshed*' as *criminal*. Yet a notice of this monstrous meeting stole into a reputable journal, thus defiantly informing the public of its illegal proceedings.

"Did the counterpart of such a gathering, to publicly applaud the assassination of our dearly beloved President, ever occur in any European country?

"Do the law-abiding of monarchical governments love their official heads less than, as a nation, we loved, as we can never love again, Abraham Lincoln? The tears of childhood still spring to our eyes when we recall the mournful tidings, flashed over the wires, which caused our parents to weep and tremble with anguish.

"We shudderingly remember the fearful events of that trying time, and now, when we are enjoying the blessings of peace, we should fully appreciate the position of other peoples who are defending their very lives against formidable conspiracies.

"Anarchy and rebellion to-day go hand-in-hand, and are composed principally of that class who believe in being supported, even to luxuries, by the labor of anyone save themselves, and are steadily advancing their dangerous sentiments, which teach that where one spends his early manhood in providing a competency for his children, dependent age, or to advance the general good, he must instead, under penalty of death, share his means with sluggards, who prefer indolence and contributory support to labor and independence.

"Could such insane doctrines be encouraged, ambition would be wiped out of every human being at one fell swoop, and we would degenerate to the indolence of the beast in the field. Progress, ambition to reach the goal by our own exertions alone, is the task set us by an all-wise Being, which extends even to fitting ourselves for a higher sphere in the life beyond."

"Speaking of the poverty of other countries," said Mrs. Penders, "I think, if we opened our eyes a tiny bit to our own vast destitution, we would be less like the deacon's little daughter who prayed, '—and, O God, bless the starving woman, with a sick babe, who fainted in the street to-day; I might have given her some of my savings, but brother says 'our *home* poor can go drown!' so immediately, dear God, I contributed all I could spare to the neglected of foreign countries. Amen.'"

"By the way, dear," questioned Mrs. Rodney, "what did your stenographer write for the coachman, O'Flanagan, in answer to his friends who asked his advice about coming to America?"

"Here is a copy of the letter," responded Mr. Rodney. "I must read it to you.

"If you have a little money to go into our western country, buy Government land and become an American farmer, with all the industry which that implies, come; there is room for millions. But if you have the same ideas which I, with all the other foolish, had, before our experience, that the crowded populace of large cities are waiting to welcome you with overrunning gold in one hand and positions of ease in the other, remain where you are in full possession of at least the latter, for outside of politics—which business is bad just now, every seat being labeled 'taken'—but one thing succeeds in America, and that is labor, mental and physical, untiring, unceasing labor; where every honest man, whose father did not do the drudgery before him, is compelled to carry out the biblical injunction, 'Thou shalt earn thy bread by the sweat of thy brow,' and rest assured not a slice more will you get than you pay for."

"Well," exclaimed Mrs. Rodney, "I did not think O'Flanagan could dictate such a sensible letter. If his friends here would follow his example, there would be fewer sufferers of his countrymen in our large cities, who left comfortable little homes, in the vain imagination that they were coming to America to pick up gold in the streets."

"Ah!" said Mrs. Penders, "O'Flanagan has learned from experience, something we must all pass through before we know the meaning of addition and subtraction. As a nation of only one hundred years old we are remarkable, yet we must not forget that we began with the full-fledged experience of our European ancestors as models, and we are not such marvelous children that we cannot still learn valuable lessons from our monarchical parents. Certainly in recompense to our public servants we are leagues behind the gratitude of European governments.

"We are still blushing over a contention of political factions who would rob the soldier of the little which is legally his. If the hades of war must come, who is entitled to greater consideration than the veteran soldiers—heroes of such martyr patriotism as the private who, when wounded, cried to the relief, 'Don't mind me—to the battle! God save our country!' and expired? The stars and stripes, preserved at the cost of two million human lives, now shelters gray and blue alike. Shall we ever upon its quivering breast write *Ingrate*,' and watch the criminal stain tearfully dripping from its folds, with the echo of its sobs wafting back to our ears 'Patriot Ingratitude'? Forbid it, God of all peoples!"

"And forgive us as a family," devoutly responded Mrs. Rodney, "for that fratricidal war! May civilized nations know wars no more, basest relic of basest barbarism!"

Mr. Rodney had resumed his paper when he excitedly read: "The White Star, which has just arrived, brings news of a burned passenger steamer at sea, the wreck being without a soul to tell the tale."

"Oh, if Tom should have been on that steamer!" said Mrs. Penders, white with fear.

"Or if poor Victoria should have been there," sadly repeated Nell Rodney.

"But if that precious Deluth could have been there," viciously added Mr. Rodney, "and perished in the flames, what a just retribution for him! But such as he always live to return to the outstretched arms of loving friends."

"I do not believe he will dare show himself here again," said Mrs. Penders.

"Why not?" sneered Mr. Rodney. "Such little eccentricities usually serve to make such a demon as Deluth quite a hero in society."

"But," indignantly remarked Mrs. Rodney, "let his poor victim, Victoria, appear, though in the most appealing penitence, she would be scorned even in her sackcloth and ashes."

"That is true," sadly replied Eunice. "I never before appreciated the partiality shown man, and the injustice which is inevitably visited upon woman. Even Mrs. Hayes deserves some consideration for her defiant conduct, after being publicly insulted by her husband."

"Yes," observed Mrs. Rodney, "you know Sibyl Hayes was a very high-spirited woman, one whom her husband should have known could be led but not driven.

"But poor cousin Vic, I can never reconcile intentional wrong with her. A more conscientious, loving girl I never knew, and she idolized her husband as surely as he did her. I could never believe her guilty, were every circumstance against her. I feel if she lives she will yet be able to clear herself. Oh, if she would only communicate with me! Surely she ought to trust me, and send me some news."

"No news is good news, Nell. I believe with you that Victoria Lennox is guiltless as a babe, and all will yet be satisfactorily cleared away. Heaven grant, for Vic's sake, it will not then be too late!

"And to think that all this misery came through the waltz, the ball-room; not as the ball-rooms were in the days of the gracefully gliding minuet; not as they could be still in the interesting and equally graceful lancers, with other decent and beautiful measures; but as the modern ball-room is —a hotbed for nurturing vice.

"Hugging to music through the seductive waltz; hugging to music through the maddening galop; hugging to music, introduced in nearly every dance now set down in the programmes of our most respectable society—no one can calculate the number of desolated homes, the parted friends, the broken hearts, the ruined lives which have occurred through this fashionable, respectably-made depravity.

"Your experience, Mrs. Penders, and that of Cousin Tom's are but two of the hundreds of similar cases constantly occurring through this astounding practice. Certainly there is suffering enough by unsuitable marriages, and the inevitable miseries which come to us unsought, without courting such temptation.

"Imagine a man deliberately looking at his mother, wife, sister, daughter or sweetheart in the arms of another man, possibly a stranger, hugging around a ball-room!

"That such familiarity is tolerated in decent society is truly appalling."

"But," questioned Mrs. Penders, "how can it and its attendant troubles be remedied?"

"I would avert a portion of this unnecessary misery by the ounce of prevention—doing away with the waltz and all hugging dances of the modern ball-room.

"Like all reforms, it would take a little

time, be sneered at, frowned down by those who cling to it; but finally, a few respectable leaders would relegate the hugging waltz to the class with whom it originated.

"Retain just as much enjoyment, and exalt self-respect by returning to the notably beautiful, graceful dances of our great grandparents, and our present numerous and equally graceful, beautiful, undulating measures."

As Mr. Rodney arose to leave for his office, he said:

"The first woman who erases from her programme and excludes from her entertainment hugging dances will be looked upon as the much-needed reformer of respectable society."

CHAPTER XI.

THE BURIAL AT SEA.

JOE JUNGLE was so nearly insane that the human kindness of the captain prompted him to separate the father from the remains of the child as speedily as possible, and therefore forced him to issue an order for its burial at sea.

It was with trepidation the second mate of the ship approached the Wayback with the decision. The officer was then surprised to hear the Wayback's reply:

"Ye couldn't have buried that body from this ship yes'day. I would o' paid millions, an' killed ye, if nusussary, but ter-day I agree to it. We'll burry the body my leetle Hank used ter live in." And the desolate father burst forth in an agony of grief.

A small saloon had been set apart for that most mournful scene, a burial service at sea.

At any time such an event casts the deepest gloom, but results of the terrible calamity to the steamer Cullard had penetrated every heart.

A few friends—made so by the late catastrophe—had been notified to assemble. The quiet which pervaded the room was truly a death stillness.

On a table lay the body of little Hank, at which one man stared with the vacant gaze of the insane. Dr. Wadsworth, who was really too ill to conduct the service, and could scarcely speak, turned to those assembled, and with deep emotion said:

"Dear hearers, before the beginning of the service our bereaved friend, Mr. Jungle, will address you. I thought better you should hear his experience and new resolves from his own lips; and I trust that in this presence of death his words will find way to your hearts and there remain."

Was that the Joe Jungle of yesterday who then arose, with pale face and gentle mien, and spoke in a mysteriously quiet tone?

"I have begged parding of the bravest men I ever see. I know God Almighty is proud of 'em. An' now I have ter say, that yes'day I wuz a big fellar.

"I thought money, that I've spent my whole life in gittin', was ever'thing. I thought I wuz big ez any God, knowed jess as much, or a great sight more; but when I felt the cold face of my boy—my boy—an' his beautiful eyes couldn't see me, an' his sweet, innercent voice couldn't say 'Pop' no more, then I knowed it was all up with Joe Jungle. I didn't 'mount to nothin'.

"All uv a sudden thar' was a great empty, achin' hole in my heart that nothin' would fill. All the geold mines of the world couldn't give me one minit's happiness. The consolation uv these kind people 'reound here"—and the Wayback's voice grew uncertain—"'specially that English lord that I hated, who saved my boy's dead body at the risk of his own life, an' the Irish parson I hated tew, an' laffed at, who jumped inter the sea ter rescue that brave woman thar'," as he pointed to Mrs. Lennox; "they've said all they could, she tew, but 'tain't no good. This airth will never be the same ag'in ter me.

"I find myself thinkin' uv some other country that I've never been tew. I feel neow that the sooner I git ter the land whar' my leetle Hank's gone, the better it'll be fur me."

"'Tain't no use puttin' on airs ag'in the God who put us here, no more'n ef we wuz leetle childurn tryin' to be wiser'n our parrents.

"All parrents love their childurn, so I've been thinkin' ef our great Father thinks a thousandth part o' me what I thinked o' my Hank, I kin trust Him that my speerit'll pan eout all right. Ef he throws this ole carcass in the ground ter rot, He'll be sure ter give me a bran' new body ter enter heaven in.

"My wife Jinnie used ter try to tell me that, and tried ter soften me, but, bless her heart, I couldn't be softened, not even by that angel of airth. She was so fine an' so like a lady, why when we wuz havin' shindigs in camp she wouldn't waltz with any one but me, she wuz so soft an' fine in her idees; not a bit like t'other women. But I couldn't 'perciate her. Wonder she ever looked at sich a' outlandish barbarian critter ez me, that nothin' would soften till leetle Hank"—tenderly pointing to the remains—"come along.

"Then thar' begun ter grow in my heart a suthin' I never knowed afore. I might be madder'n blue blazes, but let them leetle arms stretch out ter me, an' his leetle voice sound in my ears callin' 'Pop,' and I wuz a baby in a minit. I didn't b'long to myself no more, that child could take me anywhar', an' that's how I feel sence he come ter me last night in my dream.

"I could see him thar', an' I know God sent him ter console me. Thar' he stood, holdin' out his dear leetle arms an' sayin', 'Come up here, Pop; this way, this way, Pop. Mam' an' me ez waitin' fur ye, Pop. Mam's never sick no more, an' thar' ain't no poor people what starves an' cries up here.

Ever'body's happy an' waitin' fur somebody tew, jess ez me an' mam' ez waitin' fur you.'" And tears rained down the face of the Wayback as he continued:

"I tell ye what, it jess 'beout broke me up. I tried to be hard, ez I'd allers been, but 'twouldn't work no mo', an' the fust thing I knowed I wuz cryin' like a child, an' askin God, for my boy's sake, ter save a place in heaven fur me, whar' I might one day get ter jine Jinnie and Hank.

"Then all at onct my bustin' heart got light, an' a calmin' peace come ter me that I ain't knowed afore, sence I kneeled at my mother's knee an' prayed, 'Eour Father who art in heaven.'

"I tell ye what, it's the most wonderful relief anyone kin git; when ye lose all yer loved ones, an' hain't a friend on airth that kin ease the awful, achin' pain in yer heart, ter think ye kin go anywhar', even in the dark, all alone, an' find a Friend right thar', waitin' ter tell ye jess what ter du; lightens all yer burdens, promises ye shall meet yer loved ones in the beautiful home He has perpared, an' tells ye 'thar'll never be no more partin' up thar'.'

"I wish I could see all the inferdels that's spendin' thar lives tryin' ter shatter b'lief in eour great Father. I'd ask um when they pull deown the strong walls uv faith, what do they build um up with? What do they give in 'xchange fur the distruction they make? Anything? Nothin'!

"We begin ter think 'beout God when we l'arn by sufferin' an' sorrow that our joys—the leetle we do git here—is fleetin'. We jess think we've got happiness furever, an' like a child with a noo toy, we furgit anything's to come arter.

"'Long comes sickness"—and the Wayback's voice sank to a tragic whisper—"or a turrible castastrophe, an' death swoops deown on us without no warnin'. Whar' be we then? Be we so mighty big? Kin we change it? Did we know it all, or have we got ter own up that thar's a' Almighty Bein' stronger'n we be, whose ways we don't know nuthin' 'beout, no more'n leetle childurn don't know what thar lovin' parrents intend fur em?

"I hain't give this 'ere thing but a leetle study, but I kin see it all neow that I never see afore. Yes'day I thought I knowed it all, knowed more'n to b'lieve in any God; but ter-day I feel like a leetle, helpless child, toddlin' 'reound, dependent on my heavenly Father ter lead me; ter wipe away my tears; ter soothe my sufferin', bustin' heart; ter take me in His lovin' arms and quiet me ter sleep, jess as I used to my percious leetle Hank." And a flood of grief burst from the Wayback, which was shared by every listener. When he could command his voice he continued:

"Ter shatter human bein's faith in the Beyond that they've stuck ter all their life, that's upheld um like a stronger Peower; ter have that hope swept away all at onct, an' leave um alone on a desolate shore, with no thought of a sail ever heavin' in sight, ter take um home—my God! that's awful! Ev'n ter me 'twould be, an I've on'y had this faith a few heours; jess sence my boy was took.

"Thar' ain't no comfort in inferdelity fur me neow. Inferdelity will never point out the way ter them leetle arms stretched eout ter me; ter that leetle voice that I kin hear sayin', 'I'm waitin' here in heaven fur ye, Pop.'

"No! Inferdelity runs away an' hides its keoward head when death walks in; but it's then our lovin' Parrent above stands right by us; an' I neow ask Him ter save a corner inside the railin' uv heaven, anywhar', so I kin git in an' ag'in find my leetle Hank." The Wayback's tearful voice trembled, and with bursting sobs he sat down.

Mrs. Lennox, who had always shrunk from the dead, now tenderly drew aside the white pall, when all present tearfully looked a farewell at the sweet little face and then stepped back to make room for the father.

The little figure was swathed in wrappings for its watery grave, and as the father slowly approached it his staring eyes seemed ready to leap from their sockets; he pressed his lips until the blood started and his body shook with anguish. He looked steadily at the little face and then spoke.

"It's hard ter lose ye, my percious boy; it's hard, but I'd rather you went fust than leave ye alone if I wuz took." He kissed the lips while his tears rained on the little face.

"Good-by! Good-by, Hank!" he sobbed, until he was tenderly led away by Mrs. Lennox.

Dr. Wadsworth then announced that, owing to his very weak condition, he would be compelled to omit a portion of the service, and began the Episcopal burial ritual.

"'I am the resurrection and the life, saith the Lord, he that believeth in me, though he were dead, yet shall he live'"—here the Wayback interrupted with, "Oh, if leetle Hank lives neow, an' kin see me!"

The rector proceeded to the passage: "'We brought nothing into this world, and it is certain we can take nothing out. The Lord gave and the Lord hath taken away.'" The Wayback again burst forth: "Oh, if

He had took all my money an' left me Hank!"

Dr. Wadsworth proceeded to the lesson: "'For some have not the knowledge of God. I speak this to your shame. But some will say, How are the dead raised up? and with what body do they come?

"'Thou fool, that which thou sowest is not quickened, except it die: and that which thou sowest, thou sowest not that body that shall be, but bare grain, it may chance of wheat or of some other grain: but God giveth it a body as it hath pleased Him, and to every seed his own body.

"'There are also celestial bodies and bodies terrestial: but the glory of the celestial is one, and the glory of the terrestial is another.

"'There is one glory of the sun, another glory of the moon, and another glory of the stars; for one star differeth from another star in glory. So also is the resurrection of the dead.

"'It is sown in dishonor, it is raised in glory: it is sown in weakness, it is raised in power : it is sown a natural body, it is raised a spiritual body. There is a natural body and there is a spiritual body.'"

"That's it!" broke in the Wayback. "What a fool I wuz not to see it all afore."

Again the rector took up the passage : "'The first man is of the earth, earthy : the second man is the Lord from heaven. As is the earthy, such are they also that are earthy : and as is the heavenly, such are they also that are heavenly. And as we have borne the image of the earthy, we shall also bear the image of the heavenly.'"

"Ah!" sighed Joe Jungle, "how plain that is, anybody kin see it all."

Dr. Wadsworth proceeded to the verse : "'We shall all be changed, in a moment, in the twinkling of an eye, at the last trump : for the trumpet shall sound, and the dead shall be raised incorruptible, and we shall be changed.

"'For this corruptible must put on incorruption, and this mortal must put on immortality.

The Wayback infidel called in agony: "Wait fur me in heaven, Hank! Pop will come!"
(Page 137.)

"'So when this corruptible shall have put on incorruption, and this mortal shall have put on immortality, then shall be brought to pass the saying that is written, Death is swallowed up in victory.

"'O death, where is thy sting? O grave, where is thy victory?

"'Earth to earth, ashes to ashes, dust to dust.'"

As the little form was being lowered to its watery grave the heartbroken father sprang to the side of the ship and cried:

"Wait fur Pop in heaven, Hank! Pop will come! O God! take me to my boy!" And the brawny Joe Jungle swooned like a woman, in the arms of the tearful rector.

CHAPTER XII.

THE PRODIGAL.

THE sky was so beautifully blue that one could imagine a dark cloud had never veiled its brightness, nor that misery could exist in the midst of such enchanting nature, which seemed to hold for its children only beauty and love.

Eunice Penders and Nell Rodney were engaged in a most spirited conversation over the perfidy of men generally, Eunice protesting she would "never forgive" her "husband's unpardonable crime," when a servant entered with mail for Mrs. Penders. As the latter recognized the familiar handwriting of her husband, she grew faint, and begged her friend to read the letter.

Mrs. Rodney glanced through the contents to assure herself it contained nothing very scrious. Then, placing her arm affectionately around her friend, she said:

"Eunice, good news for you. Now, dear, do cease trembling, or I can never read it."

"Read it! read it!" gasped Mrs. Penders, impatiently.

"Well, dear, do control your feelings; you are so nervous," urged Mrs. Rodney, as she began the letter.

"My Darling Wife."

Here came a stifled sob from Mrs. Penders.

"Although you deem me unworthy to even write you, yet I am not what you imagine. I have only this day learned that I am supposed to be traveling with Mrs. Hayes, whom I have never seen since I left her by her husband's side that eventful night in the ball-room.

"I was a coward to insult Will Hayes, and a still greater villain to have treated you, my loved one, with disrespect.

"Mrs. Hayes, I am sure, only defied her husband through wounded pride, and regretted her impulsive act. A letter from brother Will informs me she is now with her husband.

"I have been very ill ever since I left you, and have had ample opportunity to reflect over the misery which has been brought upon me through a foolish dance.

"I fully agree with. Ned Rodney concerning the waltz. It is a physical as well as moral death to more persons than respectable society ever imagined.

"My first sickness, and one which planted in me the seeds of disease, was brought about by a severe cold taken in the ball-room.

"Barbarous treatment of one's self! From a mind-intoxicating atmosphere and burning temperature to a chilly conservatory or an icy window for a reviving breath.

"How many times have I seen a slender girl, clad only in gauze, but bedecked with glittering jewels, shudder, as the same fatal chill passed through her delicate body.

"Though very ill, I hope to reach home by the 26th of this month."

Here Mrs. Penders, who had controlled her feelings, burst into convulsive sobs, and forgetting all her wrongs, realized but one thought—her husband was ill, and she could not reach him.

Suddenly she remembered this very day was the 26th, and as she looked again at the letter, she said to her friend:

"Why, Nell, this letter came on the delayed steamer. To-day is the 26th, and

Tom, my husband, may be here—at home—perhaps *dead!*"

She rushed to her room, seized a wrap and hat, and springing through the hall, called to her friend Nell that she was "going home."

Aunt Sophronie walked slowly into the library, and, removing her gloves, sat down very quietly, with the remark: "Nell, poor Bess Darrow is dead."

"Dead!" exclaimed Mrs. Rodney, "where did you hear that?"

"I have just returned from her intimate friend, Sylvia Hawley, who received the last letter written by Bess from Paris. She had given orders to the *concierge* to forward it after her death. It is a most pathetic story; she blames waltzing for her ruin, and begs all her friends to renounce it. 'They may not follow my mad act,' she says, 'but their pure hearts will be stained by the poisonous contact of that alluring, hugging dance.'

"In the saddest manner she relates how she desired to return home to seek pardon; so, sought sympathy and advice from Mrs.

Vaintone and others, who, instead of forgiving encouragement, sneered at the poor girl's misery, denounced her as an outcast, utterly unfit to touch their own virtuous garments. Heaven help such virtue as that which permeates the robes of females like Kate Vaintone! Poor Bess Darrow never fell to the depth of that class, who, the poor girl writes, 'immediately made a hero of Walton, until that dastardly wretch, who had ruined and deserted her, was the most fêted and sought after in the American colony.' Will Darrow will be released from the asylum in a few days."

"Poor Bess! poor girl!" said Mrs. Rodney, and burst into tears.

"Ah," sighed Aunt Sophronie, sinking into one of her rhythmical inspirations—

> "By that waltz to the grave
> Po r Bess died alone,
> At last finding pardon at
> Th' Eternal's great throne.

> "Heaven welcomes the erring,
> Scorn there is unknown.
> Were her foes pure and sinless
> Who cast hardest stone?

> "Refused *her* slightest pardon,
> While *he* all forgave,
> And they still *hug* such *heroes*,
> In that waltz to the grave."

Roby and Ruby, looking the pictures of health and merriment, breathlessly entered.

"Oh, mamma," said Roby, "the wain ith gone and I ith goin' to hath a big pway to-day. Billy Withe ith comin and de ozer boys, and we ith goin' to hath dwiven horth, an' Sthock Esthange, an' libery 'table, an gwocewy thore, an eberting."

"Are you, dear?" replied his mother "I am sure you will have a lovely time, darling."

Roby, continuing his plans for the afternoon, asked:

"Mamma, muthent cook gib me eberting I want in 'e kitchen?"

"An' me, too?" pleaded his sister.

"My darlings, what do you wish from the kitchen?"

"Well," replied her son, with the most interestingly problematic air, "I wis' a board, an' a hook, an' a—an' a—oh loth o' thingths to pway wiv."

"Yat," sided Ruby, by way of urging her brother's request, "an'—an' cook won't giv' uth noffin, her thays, leth our mamma thays tho."

"That is correct, my dear. I will tell nurse to get what you wish from the large chest."

"All wight!" screamed Roby, as he joyfully ran out, exclaiming, "Youm the shtuff, mamma!"

Aunt Sophronie smiled despite herself, while astonished Mrs. Rodney called back her son to explain where he had learned such language.

"I jus' heard Walty tell hith mamma."

"What did his mother say to such a naughty expression?"

"Hers didn't say noffin," spoke up Ruby, always ready to defend her brother; "her on'y raffed."

"Only laughed!" repeated Mrs. Rodney, thoroughly horrified. "You must not play with Walter again if he uses such words;

remember, never repeat anything like that again."

"No, mamma," promised Roby, and away sped the twins to the lawn, while gallant Roby, thinking it his duty to compliment his mother on her late generous granting of his numerous requests, confided to Ruby:

"Our mamma is juth bully, ithent her?"

Ruby, as usual, seconded her brother's remark.

"Yeth, mamma ith alwayth bully."

Happy mother! Ignorance of your cherubs' compliments on this occasion is bliss indeed.

"Where," remarked Mrs. Rodney, "do well-bred children manage to learn such fearful expressions?"

"Roby told you," answered Aunt Sophronie, "that he learned his from Walter Blakely. Walter is certainly ingenious in his complimentary remarks. On the day of his mother's second marriage she confided to him that she was going to marry Dr. Blakely. Walter clapped his hands in high glee, as he whispered, confidentially:

"'Bully for you, mamma! Do the Dwoctor know it?"

Eunice Penders forgot, like many another woman, that she had firmly resolved never to forgive her husband, even were he to appeal for pardon on a suppliant's bended knee.

Is it always self-interest which makes a woman forgive where a man seeks revenge? Or is it because her heart and soul are so far above him in all nobility of character? However, she does it seventy times seven, and is then appreciated as "good nurse."

The unforgiving (?) wife, Mrs. Penders, scarcely let her feet touch the pavement, so swiftly did she fly, until she reached her handsome house, where she found only her servants.

She glanced in the parlor, she looked in the library, and finally descended to her own room. There she peered into closets, and gazed from windows, but everything seemed to echo—

"Broken vows!"

"Bleeding hearts!"

"Blighted lives!"

The hollow silence unnerved her, and as she raised her hands to shut out the visionary remembrance, she fell in a chair, brooding over the unhappy past.

In her bewilderment she was unconscious that a carriage stopped; nor did she hear the butler open the door; but starting suddenly down stairs, she saw two attendants carrying in Mr. Penders.

"My wife! my wife!" broke from the feeble man's lips as he descried Eunice hurriedly approaching him.

She fell on her knees by his side, weeping: "Tom! Tom! my own loved husband.'

The prodigal looked into the lustrous eyes of his forgiving wife, while tears fell on his pale cheeks.

"Darling, I am unworthy; but your forgiveness will lead us to brighter, happier days."

He clasped her to his heart, and inwardly breathed:

"Thank Heaven! I live to see my wife and home once more!"

Mr. Penders greeted Mrs. Rodney and Aunt Sophronie—who had been speedily summoned—with repentance, gratitude and tears, until the four friends formed a most rapturously happy weeping quartet, really pleasing to contemplate.

Mrs. Rodney and Aunt Sophronie then left to look in on other friends who might be sinking in a quicksand of misery, but, with Spartan courage, would not show it.

Aunt Sophronie ran back and peeped in, where she found the husband and wife cooing as though a cloud had never risen to mar their sunshine.

"Eunice, I forgot to advise you that though the profligate—I mean the prodigal, its all the same—has returned, not to be fooled into killing any fatted veal, but to feed him on hard tack for awhile. However, I need not have taken the trouble, for I see you are serving up the calf already. Good-by" And away she sped.

CHAPTER XIII.

LONDON.

IT was a charming suburban villa of London, surrounded by a frosty landscape. Diamond-fringed icicles bordered the artistic roof-top and glittered in the dying sunset; while from within a soft light shed its thousand iridescent hues through exquisite conceptions of stained glass.

No wonder the passer-by paused to gaze in admiration at the loveliness of the scene.

A beautiful home, we are wont to feel, is the abode of happiness; not so here. No joy pervaded this luxurious mansion. The perfume of rare exotics only breathed of a blasted life, which moaning sorrow pitifully echoed against the bars of despairing hope.

Victoria Lennox awoke from her sad reverie and touched a bell on the table by her side. Henri, the French footman, responded.

"Henri, did you deliver the note to Dr. Wadsworth which you took to the rectory?"

"No, madame," replied Henri; "I left ze note, as madame tell me, 'eef Dr. Wadsworth, be he out.' He was ze out, so I leave ze lettaire."

"That will do," said Mrs. Lennox, and Henri bowed and withdrew.

"And now," sighed Victoria, "he knows all my guilt—no, not guilt, my madness, and all my suffering for the past year. He who risked his valuable life to save mine, a worthless one. He who now begs me to become his wife. Oh, I did not mean to inspire such a feeling. I did not think it possible."

A ring at the door, which was quickly opened, admitted Charles Deluth, who without further ceremony, as usual, entered the drawing-room.

Victoria's eyes were fixed on vacancy, but as Deluth's lips touched her head she recoiled.

"Ah, my angel," said he, "dreaming again?"

"A fearful dream," responded Mrs. Lennox, "from which I never waken."

"Then I wouldn't dream," heartlessly answered Deluth. "You know Shakespeare said: 'Things without remedy should be without regard; what's done is done.'"

"But why, why," exclaimed Victoria, "when I strove to return, knowing that I was guiltless of one wrong thought, did you prevent me, until, through my insane feelings of degradation which you pictured, you carried your plans to drag my name beyond the pale of recognition? You coward, fiend!"

"Well," replied Deluth, as he threw himself into an easy chair with a cigar, "you wouldn't have me admit my failure, and be laughed at as an idiot? I offered to marry you when Jack Lennox could get his divorce, but, by George, if you didn't majestically refuse my name."

"Accept your name!" loathingly repeated Victoria; "accept anything from you, the author of all my misery!"

Deluth linked his hands across his knees,

and between the puffs of his cigar slowly answered:

"But one thing, my dear, is the matter with you. You're too awfully chuck full of sentiment: that's what made you so gullible. Superior woman in most ways, but a perfect weeping willow of sentiment. Thank heaven, I never inherited a leaf of it. I admit I deceived you, purposely deceived you, for after I once held you in my arms in the maddening waltz, I would have sold out to the very devil himself, as I would do still, to possess you.

"I knew you avoided me, shrank from me, loathed me, as you still do, and I resolved to take every advantage of that last waltz to conquer you. So far, you have vanquished me. My dear, you have not the intellectual appreciation I gave you credit for. I have been thinking all this time that you would eventually love me, if only in admiration of the diplomatic skill I evinced in winning you for that last hugging waltz. Now, instead of blaming me, you should praise me for such a *coup d'état*, and smile over the ripple you caused on the placid sea of society. When I think of the final storm we raised, I have to laugh. Ha! ha! ha!

"By the way, I received an invitation in this morning's mail, through cousin Floo, for the Roseveer reception, on the 20th of next month. By Jove! I've half a mind to go."

"You would not dare," interrupted Victoria, "go so near my husband."

"Why not?" coolly demanded Deluth. "Your husband has forgotten you, long before this; probably has another wife quite as charming as his formerly idolized Victoria.

"As to social status: when a woman, guilty or innocent, advertises her foolishness as you, unfortunately, were persuaded by me to do, her value is henceforth worthless; she will not even be accepted as a penitent, for fear comparisons might be made between the robes of compassion and the sackcloth and ashes garment.

"But with a man, little escapades of this

kind serve only to enhance his worth, and send up his stock to the highest premium. Beside, you are no common person, whose association could degrade a fellow. I am really very proud of you, wherever I go people say such nice things of my friend, 'the charming widow.' Ah! if you would only be my friend, deign to look upon me with kindness, since affection for me is impossi——"

"Charles Deluth," interrupted Victoria, "I will appeal to you once more. Will you write a truthful letter to my husband, stating my innocence, even under the cloud of guilt which you purposely spread around me? I do not care for myself; to ever meet him again were now hopeless, but I would ease his suffering, the depth of which I too well know."

"Had you treated me with kindness, even friendliness," replied Deluth, "I would have sworn to your innocence and echoed your goodness to the world, though you had sunk to blackest guilt; but after your insolent treatment of me, to confess myself fooled, beaten, an idiot—never! And I am not considered such a monster. You were supposed to know the artifices of worldly men—you were married."

"And is marriage," flashed Victoria, "a door opening into the school-room of vice, which a woman enters to be instructed by a profligate in the perfidy of his own sex? Such a type of creature was not my husband!"

"No?" interrogatively sneered Deluth. "You think him the goody-goody type, like your sleek rector, who is always dancing attendance upon you. First thing you did on the steamer was to attract the attention of that young clergyman. This is the secret of all your contemptuous conduct toward me, together with falling upon your knees in a church the moment you reached London."

"Those who conscientiously keep the halo of their church around them," sadly replied Mrs. Lennox, "will never go astray. My folly was sufficient for a lifetime of repentance. In my madness, through your counsel, fleeing like a guilty thing from the arms of a great man and loving husband to the society of a self-boasted libertine! Oh! what a leap, from heights of such perfection to such depths of degradation!"

"Too bad," sneered Deluth, "and all because of your weakness in granting me that last waltz——"

"Do not remind me of that again," cried Victoria, "for I can still feel the encircling of your slimy arms, still feel your treacherous, beating heart, still feel your hot breath poisoning your prey, even as the reptile its helpless victim."

"By Jove!" exclaimed Deluth. "If society could hear you describe the horrible effect of its enchanting waltz, fresh laurels to some of us would be difficult. The harvest it now yields would grow beautifully less. But, my dear, console yourself, you are not the first innocent victim of the intoxicating waltz, and will not be the last; many more will follow, but the fashionable world will never admit that lives are ruined through their cherished hugging dances."

Deluth had finished his cigar, and sat gazing at Victoria, now in hate, anon in admiration. At length he approached her.

"You asked me to write a letter to your husband, so that he might come here and carry you from my sight; when even to look at you occasionally is something, to me. I could write that letter, I would—" and Victoria listened eagerly for him to finish; "I would," repeated he, "if you would but be a little kind to me, and so, perhaps, assist a good action. You could compel me to this,—anything, for what was at first an unworthy passion for you has grown into a depth of love I have never known. Ah, listen," and he attempted to take her hand.

"Oh!" gasped Victoria, as she shrank from his touch.

The gleam of the devil shone in Deluth's eyes as he exclaimed, "Pah! Always your provoking sentiment. Remember, that which fascinates men of the world like me, pales on them very shortly. If you would not have me hate you, draw forth a poniard, flourish a revolver, become a very devil, but spare me sentiment."

Victoria gave one haughty look, and touched the bell on the table. "Henri, are the horses at the door?"

"Oui, madame," answered Henri.

"When the ladies of our church choir arrive, show them to the music-room, and say to them I wish to be excused to-day, but I insist that they continue their practice." And Victoria swept from the drawing-room without deigning a glance of adieu to Deluth.

"Spirit, plenty of spirit. She is the very devil to bend, but I shall bend her finally. I was never yet beaten in my race for a woman. Death is the only thing which could make me give her up now. Ha! ha! Victoria; having waited so long, I can wait longer." He looked at his watch. "Still an hour before dressing for dinner. I will improve a portion of it listening to the ladies of the choir. Wonder if they've any pretty women among them?" As he thought of going to the music-room in advance of the ladies' arrival, he heard the voice of Joe Jungle speaking to Henri. "Ah," thought Deluth, "I will talk to the Wayback."

CHAPTER XIV.

THE NEW JOE JUNGLE.

"GONE ridin'? Wall, I'll jess wait till she comes back, ef she ain't gone more'n a' heour. O, Meester D'luth, how du yeou du?" as he shook hands with Deluth. "I ain't seen you afore in quite a while. What business be ye in neow?" And Joe Jungle sat down, quite at home.

Deluth, amazed that anyone should not see that he was far above a profession or business of any sort, haughtily replied: "I am not building churches, at all events."

"No, I guess not, that ain't in your line; nur writin' Bibles, uther."

"I leave such occupations for fools, who haven't brains for anything sensible," quickly answered Deluth.

"Oh, what, may I ask, do your sensible folks du?"

"Well, they manage to get along without any of your foolery, believing in a future life and a God, sailing around somewhere, instead of relying on themselves. As though any being could exist greater than mortal man." And Deluth assumed an attitude befitting an emperor of the universe.

"Guess you must know Wongersol, of York. He's 'nuther big 'mortal man.' Las' time I heerd him he wuz makin' hundurds uv people laff 'beout the Almighty. I couldn't help thinkin' Dan Rice, the circus clown, wuz nowhar' in comparison. Me an' my friends laffed tew, with t'other ones. I didn't know no better then, that's why I wuz thar'. I wuz goin' whar' thar' wuz any fun on hand, an' I usually managed in sich places as that ter strike a class that wuz 'beout ez ignurant ez I wuz, exceptin' sometimes some people got in thar' by mistake. One night I see a man an' woman at the box office arter their money, said they didn't buy a ticket for a 'burlesque Artemus Ward performance.' The inferdel actor sums himself up in 'beout these words: 'I deon't b'lieve nuthin' I ken't see, hear er grab onto. Thar' ain't no God, else He'd taken me—Wongersol—inter His confidence, told me all He'd ever done, an' ever intended doin', then I might o' told Him how to run things different.'

"Ef some people hadn't l'arned suthin', an' others got 'shamed goin ter hear him, the biggest inferdel egotist this world has ever produced would have ordered a' Eiffel Tower ladder, an' by this time been up in the cleouds, play actin' the Almighty hisself, an' advertisin': 'Special performance! A dollar a head.'"

Deluth was interested; he thought, "This Wayback is a queer genius; I'll lead him on."

"Well, what do you think of the Bible racket?"

"What do ye mean by the Bible racket?" repeated Joe Jungle.

"Why, the nonconformity of its writers, the mistakes or lies of the history."

"Wall, that makes me think uv a mine I had; it wuz named Joe Jungle, arter myself. I wanted it writ up in the papers, so I engaged four newspaper men ter du it. They wuz from York, Chicago, St. Louis an' 'Frisco. They took a hasty look at the mine, and pitched in; but some of um got East fur West, an' North fur South; some said it 'was gravel bed' whar' 'twas rock; 'nother said 'it was red sand,' an' 'nother said ''twas all three.' Anyhow, each feller writ his description ez he understood it, an' some of um interduced a lot o' poet idees, jess like the al'gories uv the Bible, but it wuz writ good, an' I knowed it, an' I sold the mine fur sever'l million.

"Then the paper men come fur their pay es agreed on; I thought I'd have a little fun with um, an' sez I, 'But none o' you fellers described that mine alike, every one o' ye made meestakes,' an' I told whar'. Then they all runned down ter the mine ag'in, an' looked. Everyone on um admitted he wuz wrong in locatin' an' lots o' details—got it kinder twisted reound, but one on um says, says he, 'Wall, neow, look o' here, Meester Jungle, gittin' the location a leetle wrong, er sayin' gravel fur rock, or flingin' in poet pictur's, didn't hurt it, nur your chances; you sold the mine jess the same, an' ye know we all four writ it jess as we understood it, and in the main we was right, wa'n't we?' 'Yes,' says I, 'an' by that I sold the mine, an' I didn't cheat nobody; it wuz wo'th every dollar I got fur it. Here's yer money, boys, an' a hundurd to boot; ye writ it good, fust rate, an' yer meestakes wa'n't nothin', fur ye all agreed in the main. Ef ye du everything as well an' honest in life, ye'll pan eout all right.'

"Neow, so it wuz with the Bible writers: some uv um writ kind o' al'gories, that's the poetry writin' way some uv them paper men writ 'beout my mine. It's more natural to some ter writ in the soarin' poetry kind, an' some others ken writ better'n the plain, hard-pan talk; they're jess ez good, one as t'other, fur different people. Then ag'in, ye know, lots o' things have got changed in translatin', made the meanin' of some words very different from what they wuz just writ er intended; but the inferdels needn't be 'larmed their bible'll ever suffer by translatin,' fur 'nuff uv it won't never live to meet with any sich flatterin' accident.

"The poet writers make me think of people who must have fleowers on their eatin' tables, ter give um a' appetite; others ag'in couldn't eat if thar' wuz a fleower 'round, less it wuz in the shape of boiled cabbage, an' had corned pork vines trailin' 'reound it.

"I wuz almost ez bad ez that myself onct," and the Wayback heaved a sigh. "I'm deeferent neow. Don't kneow how it is, but I'm deeferent in every way since little Hank wuz took. Why, ter think uv Joe Jungle lookin' at fleowers; didn't kneow one from t'other, an' neow I ken sit and talk ter the beautiful leetle blossoms our heavenly Father grows in this world fur the pleasure uv His childurn.

"Who can look at a leetle fleower, an' not thank the loving friend, the Great Artist, who paints um for us an' sends um to blossom right at eour feet?

"Tell ye what, it's on'y great heroes, er

kings an queens, er weddin' pairs, who git fleowers strewed in their path. We could never show such delicate thoughtfulness to eour children, even to the greatest favorite; an' here God sends um to His sons and daughters, good an' bad, all alike," as he looked at Deluth, "tew you tew—the wo'st in the world ken find a beautiful fleower at his feet, breathin' a message of love from its Maker.

"I don't see how sich a' ignurant creetur' as a' inferdel lives in this beautiful world. It don't take no l'arnin', an' but leetle understandin' to see that there is a great Creator, who rules the mighty universe an' arranges ever'thing. Why, we need on'y look in the sky, at the sun, moon, an' stars, which the greatest scientists hev never reached, nur Wongersol hez ever jerked deown; then come ter airth, an' examine a leetle buttercup growing in a pasture; one's jess as big a mystery as t'other; we've never feound eout what either one was made from, an' have never seen the wonderful Manufacturer. Yet Wongersol'll tell ye thar' ain't no

Being greater than mortal man, an' expects ye to b'lieve him, while he tells ye a good joke to make ye swaller it quick, without thinkin'.

"Ef a man or woman l'arns suthin' right well, they allers know they've got ter give a hull lifetime ter that one thing, whether its farmin', minin', manufacturin', skeowl-teachin', paintin', er politics.

"Jess think how leetle 'tis we ken du; then compare our leetle imitation 'complishments with the Bein' who superintends all the machinery uv this great airth; who looks arter all the billions uv gardens, sends sun an' rain ter make the billions uv food stuff an' the beautiful things ter grow, fur our nuscussities, an' happiness; feeds the billions uv fish in the sea, the billions uv cattle on the land, the billions uv birds in the sky, the billions uv beasts uv the forest, the billions uv human bein's, His children, an' all conducted like the tickin' uv a clock, er a perfect reg'lated household.

"Then ter think a person ever lived who was so sick'nin' vain foolish as ter compar' his leetle minikin imitations to that uv our Creator. Why, they don't desarve ter live an' be rec'nized by thar brothers an' sisters, on'y that our heavenly Father don't make no deestinction, an' tells us ter 'love one 'nother.' Why, the biggest thing we ever done is on'y imitations of the Great Teacher.

"Awhile ago, I wanted ter buy a fine Turner pictur' fur Mrs. Lennox's birthday prusunt, but 'twas sold. The pictur' man told me he'd git me 'a copy painted fur twentieth the price, but uv course the name uv the great artist wouldn't be on it, as 'twould be on'y a copy.' So I told him I didn't want no copies. Then he said, 'Uv course the 'riginal would allers demand a big sum uv money, cuz the name of the artist would live furever.'

"Last week I went tew a' artist show, an' ever'body was strainin' thur necks ter see some pansies that the artist Dupray painted. I ricollicted I hed some pansies in a paper fur Mrs. Lennox, so I jess slid um right up near the kenviss an' looked. The imitation wuz mighty good, but it fell short when compar'd to the nateral fleower.

"The next day I noticed all the papers I read spoke uv the great artist, said he wuz the 'greatest fleower painter ever lived.' The pictur' wuz sold fur big money; but nobody thought that, arter all, 'twa'n't o'ny a copy uv the pansies he had afore him to paint from. No one, not even the fleower painter, thinked of the wonderful Artist Teacher, who sent him all the beautiful colors ter use—his heavenly Father—who made the real, 'riginal, nateral pansies grow."

Deluth wished to hear the Wayback further, but Joe Jungle subsided into a deep, thoughtful mocd, to arouse him from which Deluth propounded another question, one which at that moment seemed to weigh upon him.

"Mr Jungle, do you think a loving God would permit his children to suffer, as they do in this world, mentally and physically?"

Joe Jungle looked up quickly. "Would we 'preciate health ef we were never sick; light, ef not darkness; happiness, ef not sadness; an' so on? I guess God knows what He's 'beout.

"Makes me think of a docter and his little son, that came to camp a few year sence. The boy in playin' 'reound machinery got his leg mashed flat, so the father had ter cut it off ter save the boy's life. I tell ye it made the men feel queer ter hear that little feller beg his father not ter cut his leg off. 'Oh, father,' he cried, 'I'd rother die than have my leg cut off! Don't do it, I'd rother die.' I could never furgit that docter, ez he stood by his boy, with white face an' streamin' eyes, an', says he, 'My son, I want ter save yer life; it will hurt, my boy, but 'twill save yer life, an' ye'll be dearer ter me than ye ever was afore. Let me save yer life, an' then I can take ye home. My percious boy, trust yer father that he'll see ye through all right.' There wa'n't no chlorofo'm, ethur, or nuthin' the docter could get in time, so the little boy had ter submit, an' he done it like a sojier.

"The great drops of sweat runned off his pale for'head like rain, while his father cut inter his flesh, an' sawed through his bones, but he stood it without a cry. The leg wuz burried in the greound an' left ter rot; 'twa'n't no good ter the boy no mor'n our bodies be when we put um in the greound fur a spiritual body in heaven.

"In a few months, when the boy got well, he put his arms 'reound his father's neck, an' said, 'Father, I'm glad you cut my leg off, an' didn't let me die; you knowed best, an' neow you're goin' ter take me home.'

"His father pressed him to his heart, an' said, 'Yes, my brave boy, we are now goin' home.' That's the kind uv faith we need in eour Creator—free from all inferdelety, from all distrust. Jess obey Him like obedient children, an' leave all the rest to eour heavenly, lovin' Parrent, who'll see that we pan eout all right."

"Don't you think," said Deluth, as he admiringly stroked his silken mustache, "it is too bad to destroy a beautiful body by putting it in the ground to decay? Why could we not as well be translated, body and soul, as Elijah was?"

"Neow, that makes me think," replied the Wayback, "uv the figur' Mrs. Lennox made uv my leetle Hank. I see it fust in clay, an' yesterday I see it ag'in in bronze. I told her that I'd pay fur the clay 'riginal, as I wanted ter perserve it tew; but she told me a' artist never kept the clay model, 'twa'n't good fur nothin' when the mould was made from it, 'cause the clay all fell ter pieces gittin' the noo figur'.

"Thar' ag'in, I thought, that's like my leetle Hank's body, left in the sea; 'twa'n't no good ter th' Almighty when he got through with it, 'cause He give him 'nother body.

"I'm l'arnin' suthin' ever' day, an' lookin' back, I wonder I couldn't see it afore; but then I wuz so ignurant. But what 'stonishes me is that people who have a chance uv seein' an' thinkin' sh'u'd ever git so conceited ez ter say they know it all, an' ruther than give up their 'tarnel vanity, an' own they don't know nuthin', they'll try ter make b'lieve thar' ain't no God. I pity sich pursens, 'cause that wuz the way with me.

"I'm jess goin' to build a temple fur sich poor heathen, an' exhibit specimens of God's beautiful works; an' chuck in plenty of books of l'arnin' fur the inferdels, an' give 'em a life ticket to come an' practice in a big laboratory, er eny other department, an' I'll give eny man er woman a million dollars who thinks thar' ain't any Being greater than they be, who'll tell me uv any manufacturer who kin make a grain o' seed from which a tree will greow, er restore life to even a leetle dead bird. Guess they'll find that God give Himself a patent on all His works, an' the most He's ever 'lowed mortal man ter du is ter make a copy uv some uv um."

CHAPTER XV.

JOE JUNGLE ADOPTS A DAUGHTER.

DELUTH'S time was up, and being engaged to dine out, he departed for his hotel to dress.

As Victoria had not returned from her drive, Joe Jungle decided to keep an appointment with a mining camp friend and then return to the Lennox mansion.

No sooner had he gone than Rev. Dr. Wadsworth appeared at the door, with beaming countenance, and nervously rang the bell.

"Ah," thought the happy rector, "if it is heaven's will that I gain this blighted flower, I will transplant it to a garden of sunshine which shall never know shadow while I live. It seems but yesterday that I rescued her from ocean's grave. She received my letter, telling her all my hopes, and she has not forbidden me to come for her answer. It must be all my heart's desire; moments are years until I call her mine."

So wrapped in visions of happiness was the rector he did not observe that Henri, the footman, stood quietly holding open the door, and with the faintest suspicion of a concealed smile on his usually precise countenance.

Dr. Wadsworth, still in dreamland, took no notice of Henri, but sprang to the drawing-room. Henri's smile widened considerably, as he respectfully followed and waited until the rector had returned to earth sufficiently to ask for Mrs. Lennox. When informed she was not at home the rector grew ghastly pale. Henri, who understood the situation, thought he would depart from his usual course, and volunteered the information:

"Monsieur le Pasteur, madame send to the rectore one lettaire to-day. I take him about four hours' time."

"You took a letter to the rectory four hours ago?" questioned Dr. Wadsworth.

"Oui, Monsieur le Pasteur," replied Henri.

This did not comfort Dr. Wadsworth, but he hastily remarked: "I left home about that time to officiate at the wedding of a parishioner living some distance in the country. I came direct from there here. Say to your mistress that is why I did not receive her letter." And away he darted, in the same wild manner he had entered, still hoping to receive welcome news through the little missive.

Henri's situation in the household of Mrs. Lennox suited him too well to wish a change; he was therefore more pryingly watchful than servants generally are—if that were possible—of all which transpired within the Lennox domain. He now soliloquized.

"Monsieur le Pasteur very nice, but he craze to teenk madame evair maree he. I see ze lettaire he send to she. Oh! so mooch ze loav eet make my heart go zhumps way up. He nice, but I no like to go to ze rectore to leev, an' I no like to leaf madame. But she no maree, I seenk she haf mooch trouble here," and he touched his hand to his heart, just as a ring at the door vibrated upon his sensitive ear.

No sooner did Victoria learn that the rector had called than she hastily questioned Henri, "Did Dr. Wadsworth leave any message?"

"Oui, madame. Monsieur le Pasteur, he say he leaf ze rectore four hours' time to offecate at one of hes parish who die—no, who maree"—all same thought Henri, as he gave his shoulders a suggestive shrug; "zat ees why he no get ze lettaire madame send me to he."

Mrs. Lennox gave a sigh of relief at not having seen the rector; and had just dined when Mr. Jungle was announced.

While the would-be groom sat in the drawing-room waiting the appearance of Mrs. Lennox, he mused: "I deon't know heow I'm goin' ter start in; wonder ef she see that I've been courtin' of her fur some time neow? I ain't got but little edication—but then she's got 'nuff fur both on us; she deon't go much on money, but I've got slathers uv it, an' money talks neow'days, ez well in crowned-head deestricks ez in the United States of Amerikay, whar' b'ilin' soap hez sent many a man ter Congriss; en eout here barrels o' money—bottlin' steout —hez made lords uv the bottlers. That shows progriss that's right ez long ez a man does some good with his dollars, instid uv devotin' his last breath to ceountin' an' huggin' um like a miser. In that way he deon't du no good, nur enjoy life.

"The youngsters at scheool that eat thar kendy an' oranges without dividin' with th' others, got ever' bit uv th' oranges an' kendy, sure 'nuff, right inter thar own leetle stomachs, but it didn't do um much good, fur they didn't smile an' look happy like the boys and gurrls who devided all 'reound.

"Wall, I don't kneow how tew start in. The parson, uv course, would du the tyin' uv the knot, right shinin', all dressed up in his geown an' best bib an' tucker. I'll kind o' git 'reound it, talkin' 'beout the parson an'——."

His meditation was checked by the entrance of Mrs. Lennox, whom he welcomed most effusively, after which he gradually worked up to the desired point.

"Mrs. Lennix, ye kneow you an' me an' the parson hez been 'quainted some time neow, an' we understan' one 'nuther purty well, I reckon. Neow, the rector is varry fond uv you, an' he'd only be tew happy to du it up breown."

Misconstruing his meaning, Victoria was alarmed, thinking the rector had confided to others, and decided to hush up the matter quickly. Joe Jungle, however, interrupted her thoughts.

"The parson's been lookin' kind o' shy at me ever' time he feound me 'reound here lately; so I jess concluded I'd speak tew you 'fore he asked you 'beout it."

"O dear! Mr. Jungle, I did not imagine the rector had made a confidant of anyone. I beg that you will silence the breath of any such rumor, as I now tell you confidentially, I have declined the hand of Dr. Wadsworth."

"No!" gasped Joe Jungle, as he suddenly realized that if Mrs. Lennox would not accept the rector, there certainly was not the ghost of a chance for an inferior.

"Yes," continued Victoria, "I feel deeply that I should be placed in a position to refuse so small a favor as the bestowal of my hand to that brave man who saved my life at the risk of his own valuable existence. I would give that life now to spare him pain. I so regret he should have had a feeling of affection for me, as that circumstance renders it impossible to continue our friendship. I must never meet him again. I loved but one man, him I married. I shall *never* love another, or marry again."

No one who heard the sad but decisive tones of Victoria could doubt for one moment that it were impossible to change her views. Joe Jungle drew a long breath, as he almost thought aloud:

"So it's the parson; I kinder thought I smelt a mice when he wuz 'reound, but 'twas his own love-makin' he looked shy 'beout. Glad I went sleow. Come mighty near puttin' my foot in it. 'Twould o' hurt her feelin's ter refuse me tew, an' then she'd never see me no more neither, jess ez she won't the parson. I couldn't b'ar that. Without knowin' it, she's wound herself reound my heart strings so tight, they'll never come off without cuttin' eout the heart. I'll have ter fix it some way."

"Wall, Mrs. Lennix, I'm awful sorry 'beout the parson, an' 'taint no good ter advise anyone who feels like you do. But I've been thinkin' strong, uv late, that you need a pertector, someone that's got the right "—Victoria threw up her hands in alarm—" yes, a pertector. Neow, sence you've refused the parson, I'm goin' ter perpose ter you——"

"Oh!" gasped Victoria, "I beg you will not compel me to refuse——"

"Ter be my dawter?" interrupted Joe Jungle, laughing.

Victoria's face changed into a beaming smile, while she replied: "Oh, what a burden you have taken off my heart! I began to think—you meant—something serious, and I should be compelled to renounce your friendship also."

"An' ter be my dawter ye won't never have ter du that. Ye see, I've got tew much money, an' I want a wife—I mean, a dawter—ter sit right deown an' direct me what ter du with it."

"Do you believe," smilingly responded Victoria, "in a woman as business director?"

"Wall I should remark. Most on um kin see further with their eyes shut than the sharpest men kin with both eyes open. Why, ef it hadn't been fur my wife Jinnie, I'd sold the Jungle mine fur nothin'; but Jinnie kept sayin', 'Neow, Joe, thar's suthin' in that mine, I know; en' ef ye won't keep it fur yerself, keep it fur me.'

"A year arter, I sold it fur nine million, the same mine Jinnie made me keep when I was achin' ter trade it fur a jackknife an' a hobby-horse.

"A real bright woman's got a way uv seein' right through suthin' she knows nuthin' 'beout, an' kin see it all 't once. Guess you're a purty good manager. You run this heouse, yeour hired help, an' tend to yer own bankin' and stock business all yerself. Don't ye?"

"Yes," replied Victoria, in so sad a voice that Joe Jungle thought he had caused her to think of the time when she had a husband to do all that, and he was right. Jack Lennox, the deserted, seemed to stand, in reproach, by her very side. "I have no one," continued she, "whom I would permit to look after any of my financial affairs, as I personally attend to everything."

"I knowed it," replied Joe Jungle. "Women air, nine-tenths the time, the great motive peower behind the biggest money-barrels. Ef she wore pants an' smeoked cigars she'd git a big sal'ry for the 'meount uv seound advice she turns eout; but as 'tis she deon't make a cent as business adviser. Ef 1 couldn't adopted ye, I'd o' tried ter hire ye; but now ye'll turn adviser ter me in ever'thing

"Ter-morrow we'll have the papers made eout in legal form. Then you'll be my dawter, Victoray Lennix Jungle—Jungle deon't seound right, does it? Wall, fur your sake, we'll leave off the Jungle from yer kerds, but ye'll be my dawter all the same, an' ever'thing I hev in th' world b'longs right ter you, an' ye'll find it all fixed that way ef I go fust."

"Why, the poor gurrl deon't hear one word I say. I've set her to thinkin' 'beout poor dead Lennix, I s'pose, that's jess like me; if I keep on she'll never sign the 'doptin' papers ter be my dawter. Neow I've got her into this deownhearted way, I must do suthin' to raise her speerits, but I ain't 'lectual 'nuff ter talk real brainy book stuff."

The Wayback gazed tenderly at Mrs. Lennox, who seemed unconscious of all surroundings; her eyes had that far-away expression which always told they were looking three thousand miles beyond the sea. He was wild to know how to divert her thoughts. Suddenly he began:

"Say, Victoray; Victoray is a purty name; I didn't used to dream uv it till I see you. Sence then I'm either thinkin' uv you er the Queen. S'pose we call on the

Queen an' invite her ter take dinner at eour house, an' we'll have fireworks arter. I'll tell her I've jess had a dawter and sheow her you. I'll git Oakdale ter interduce us,—oh, she'll be glad ter have us come, she likes him. An' I like her, jess 'cause she wuz named arter you. I should hev hed Oakdale take me there afore, on'y I thought ef I went there much th' Englishmen might git mad, thinkin' I wuz steady company and hankerin' like ter leadin' of her to th' altar.

"Ye know the Queen's a widow, an' I'm a widower.

"I s'pose she's refused lots uv men here, an' they know ef I be a' eout an' eout American, I've got lots uv money, 'nuff ter buy all the palaces she wants; but even ef I hadn't been in love with some other Victoray—my dawter—I wouldn't asked the Queen noheow, for I never would hev my wife work fur a livin', with all the money I've got; an' she'll never giv up her old position in the palace eout uv respect ter th' English that fust offered her the place; an' they've got so 'customed to her, it would kind o' shake up the British heousehold ter part with her neow.

"Well, she's got a good sit, anyway, an' for life; 'way ahead uv eour Prusidunt, who's, arter all, a kind o' he-queen to a Republic, on'y we beounce um every four year, don't give um no sich pay, 'an never think uv lovin' um like the people eout here du the Queen, an' we've got jess ez many starvin' poor in perportion.

"We've hed some good he-queens—I mean Prusidunts,—but they ain't all been George Washingtons er Abraham Lincolns, not by a long sight; but I guess the world'll shake hands with England when she says the best sovereign she's ever hed sits right on her throne neow.

"Ye see, Queen Victoray begun all right. She was a bright, brainy woman ter start with, an' she went right on ter a lovin', devoted wife an' mother—all of um the best faults a woman could have.

"I didn't used ter know nothin' 'beout her till I found out she had such samples of brave men as Lord Oakdale."

Here the Wayback's voice suddenly ceased, he looked upward, as though communing with little Hank, then recalled himself and proceeded.

"I used ter dispise any country that hadn't a Prusidunt, but I find thar' be other people who git along purty well an' pay all their debts, even ef they don't chuck the head uv their nation eout o' office every four year. Jess ez ef we war afraid they'd steal 'nuff to bankrupt the gover'ment ef they stayed a minit longer; but I never knowed a' honest one yet, ef he took the job uv Prusidunt, to have 'nuff when he left the White Heouse ter build a log cabin.

"I kinder guess the people who 'lect their head fur life gits 'long 'beout ez well. Anyhow, it saves a deal of cartage an' whitewashin' money, to say nothin' uv the heap it costs fur mendin' carpets, gluin' the furniture, buyin' more crockery, fryin' pans, kittles, an' bedquilts every four year.

"There ain't much 'conomy in that, but, 'Never mind 'xpenses,' says t'other party; 'it's our turn to have a whack at politics, and we'll boost ye sky high.' So they collect a few millions, which they promise ter pay back out o' the people's money when they git inter office, and perceed 'to boost.'

"The pollin' wheel turns, an' sometimes a' honest man is drawed, an' sometimes he ain't. Whichever way it goes, we've got ter grin an' b'ar it fur 'nother four year.

"I thought monarchies ought ter be l'arned suthin' by us, but I guess they kin paddle their own canoe, ez they've done ten times the centennials to the one we've hed.

"Sence I've looked 'reound here in fureign lands, an' see ever'thing so well took care uv fur the last thousand year, I often think kinder ser'us whar' we'll be in ten more centerries, if we don't mind some of our p'litical mashshinery and sodder up bad leakages.

"Ez fur our Prusidunt, ez I wuz sayin' afore, he don't no more'n git in an' git 'quainted with the gover'ment book he's tryin' ter straighten eout, than he's told his 'time's up' an' he'll have ter leave the rest fur the incomin' superintendent, that knows as little 'beout it as he did when he was took in.

"He ain't 'tall satisfied with a hundurd things he hadn't time ter add up an' subtract, but no matter 'beout that, the other fellow's been hired fur the place, and th' expressman sticks his head in the door an' yells, 'Hurry up with yer boxes.'

"I kin see him stick his pen 'hind his ears and rush upsta'rs to his wife.

"She's feedin' a teethin' baby in her lap, and tryin' ter quiet another youngster who wants to go out ridin' in the rain. But the ex-Prusidunt is so crazy blind he ken't see nothin', so he screams to her like a house afire:

"'Mary Ann! thar' you're sittin' doin' nothin'. The movin' van's here, an' the men sw'arin' a blue streak at keepin' um waitin' s'long. Neow, jess hustle areound! No time ter pack nothin' else! Jess throw them things inter baskets an' borrels, an' let us git out o' here 'fore the noo folks git back from 'nauguration.

"'I'm blamed sorry I ever gave up clerking in my little teown ter come here an' be 'bused fur a few months, an' then be kicked out jess ez if I'd been stealin'.

"'Never mind them silks, laces an' things o' yourn, or the young ones' clothes; chuck um in anywhar'.

"'Whar's my best breeches? I'll need um to wear to church when we git back to Kalamazunk to be star'd at; long time 'fore I ken 'ford 'nother pa'r. My high hat tew, be awful kerful o' that, an' fold all my things nice an' smooth.

"'Now du hustle! you've been up sence four o'clock this mornin' an' ain't done a thing but git breakfast. Why on airth didn't ye hire a woman to help ye ter-day, and hang the expense?

"'I've been workin' like a hoss all mornin' thinkin' about that affair at Town Hall, whar' I was fool enough ter go into jess four year ago an' take th' oath uv office. What a' ass I was, anyway!

"'Fou'th o' March! Fine time o' year ter ask a civilized man ter move his family, with teethin' youngsters tew. Anyheow, I'm glad ter git out o' this White House. Had malary ever sence they put me in here, that's what makes teethin' so hard fur the baby. We may bless our stars we ain't all dead. Place is full o' rats, tew; rotten old hole.

"'Goodness gracious! hear them movin' men sw'ar at us fur keepin' um waitin'.

"'Mary Ann, don't furget ter make a memorandum of the things ye give the cartmen, er they'll say we "stole a lot when we moved." The gov'ment needn't be 'larmed 'beout me. Ain't a 'tarnel thing I'd have in the old rat-trap ef they'd give it to me.

"'Neow, never mind the youngsters, let um yell. Have ye give the dog an' cat thar breakfust? The cat's mewin', poor thing; she's sorry I'm goin'. She'll git nothin' but starved mice ter live on when we're gone, an' she knows it. See how pitiful she looks at me—git her suthin t'eat, quick!

"'Now, hurry up, I'm goin' deownsta'rs to see ef I've left any change in the safe; ef I ain't, you'll have to bu'st open the childurn's tin banks to git money 'nuff to pay fur movin', fur I ain't got a cent in my pocket;

I give the last dollar to the butcher an' confectioner on 'count them 'xtra dinners we give to the second term galoots who said I was 'all right fur nuther four year.' I knowed they hadn't a' ounce o' sense, one on 'em.

"'Hark! what kerriage is that rattlin' an' stopped here ter-day, I'd like ter know? Wall! hang his imperdence, ef it 'tain't t'other feller. 'Taint on'y twenty minutes past twelve, an' here he has galloped up the street ez ef he was 'fraid I'd take the White House with me; wall, he's got gall. It was thirty-five minutes of one, wa'n't it, Mary Ann, 'fore we took possession the day we moved here? But some people air swine anyway, an' ther's no kinder use puttin' pearls 'reound their necks an' expectin' perliteness of um.

"'Come here, Mary Ann, an' see the gang git out the kerriage. That noo fellar looks like a footman, don't he? No dignity 'beout him, is thar'? How could thar' be, he's such a stumpy little pigmy.

"'What de ye say, "two inches taller'n

me"? Mary Ann, you're a fool! I've noticed you couldn't see straight ever sence las' 'lection.

"'Don't go 'way; come back here an' see um; come an' look at his wife's green bunnet. Ha! ha! I thought that 'u'd fetch ye. Look at th' young ones, an' all uv um stare at eour house; they look ez ef they thought we wa'n't goin' to give it up.

"'Thar'! hear um ring the front door bell ez ef they'd jerk the handle off; shows heow they've been brought up; kerries out what I've said of um ever sence he beat me on the second term. Ring away! ring away! Guess they'll be 'stonished to find all the servants gone lookin' fur noo places.

"'Ringin' again! Well, I s'pose I'll have ter let um in. Neow, du hurry up, Mary Ann, an' git the things all packed nice, an'— Stop ringin' that bell! Deon't kneow heow ter ring a decent bell. Stop ringin', I say! I'm comin' deownsta'rs ez fast ez I ken, but jiss understand in advance ye don't own the White Heouse, an' ye ken't put me eout o' here 'fore one o'clock P.M.'

"Ha! ha! That's abeout what movin' day is at the White Heouse, an' we uv the United States call the office uv Prusidunt a soft snap.

"I'm glad I made ye laff ag'in, Victoray—my dawter."

Mrs. Lennox, who had forgotten the proposed new relationship, looked suddenly surprised, then changed into a smile of remembrance.

"I tell ye, I'm a' American from wayback; but sence I crawled eout o' my shell in the minin' deestrick an' traveled, I kin 'preciate heow awful ignorant I wuz, by learnin' how much I deon't know neow. I reckon I'm jiss 'beout like the other folks who hev ter travel ter git rid o' thar prujidices an' see that all edicated people, in thar senses, air' 'beout alike, whither they're fureign er uv home-made breedin'.

"'Tain't long sence most Americans thought fureigners did nothin' greater than w'ar one eyeglass, drive tandem, an' 'buse thar poor.

"An' afore fureigners traveled in eour

parts, they s'posed we wore a headgear uv peacock feathers, hung jewels in eour noses, an' danced war-whoops b'fore bonfires as a religi's exercise.

"Neow you're lookin' a little pleasanter. I'm goin' ter leave ye so ye kin git rested, an' be bright fur ter-morrow, ter sign the 'doption papers. No, ye can't say nothin' neow, and thar ain't no foolin' 'beout this, neither."

"Oh, if you knew how I had sinned, though unintentionally; how through mad folly my name is blackened, you would not offer me the tender protection of a parent," said Mrs. Lennox.

"Ef you've sinned an' suffered, so much the better fur you; ye won't hev ter suffer over fur that same mistake; 'cause ye'll know more'n ter make it ag'in. 'Tain't nucessary fur ter tell me you did it unknowingly; ef 'twas wrong, you bet you didn't mean ter du it.

"I wouldn't b'lieve you did, ef ye told me that yourself. I've kneowed you more'n a year, an' you're alwers charitable ter other folks. Why kent ye hev a little fur yerself? Don't ye know charity sheould begin at hum'?

"I've watched ye ever sence yeur tender hands took the cloth from Hank's little dead face," and the Wayback stopped, overcome with emotion, coughed and resumed. "An' ef you know anyone that thinks they're better'n you be, jiss tell um what The Man said, three thousand year ago, ter the set o' critters tryin' to mob a woman:

"'Let any one on ye that's ez good ez she is threow the fust stone.' I notice none on um threowed it; they wuz 'fraid Jesus intended to compar' characters, an' they purty quick dropped their rocks an' slunk away.

"Good-night, my dawter. Heaven bless ye."

Victoria's grateful, bursting heart tremblingly whispered, "Good-night—father!" and the adopted daughter was enfolded in the honest arms of Joc Jungle.

CHAPTER XVI.

THE RECTOR.

JOE JUNGLE departed, proud of his paternal recognition.

The ladies of the choir, who had delayed their rehearsal until evening, had now arrived, and were conversationally discussing composers in the music-room.

Victoria had scarcely recovered from feelings of gratitude for the delicate human sympathy offered her by the Wayback, when Henri announced the rector.

"No! no!" said Mrs. Lennox, at once thoroughly alarmed; "say to Dr. Wadsworth I beg he will excuse me;" and as Henri left the room Victoria fell in a chair, shivering at the bare thought of being in danger of again meeting the rector. Suddenly a voice aroused her:

"May I not come to you?" he faintly pleaded.

"No! no! I cannot look on your face again; be merciful, leave me!"

Notwithstanding, the almost tottering form of the handsome young rector approached her.

"Ah, that letter!" he gasped; "it has crushed me, broken my life!" and he sank in a chair by the side of Mrs. Lennox. "Yet something is left me: I would not exchange that wealth of holy love I have borne and will ever bear for you, for all this earth could offer me. That love throughout my life will be my deepest sorrow—but my greatest joy.

"Perhaps this affliction has been wisely sent me. I have heretofore been too harsh in judging human weakness. I never appreciated until now that attachments may lead to the highest plane of happiness, or consign to a living death, making of our lives such a penitential agony as can be known only to ourselves and to our God. I can now understand wherein I have lacked sympathy with those who have suffered through their affection, which, too, is the secret of so many unhappy marriages.

"Without love, marrying from some force of circumstance—marrying for position—marrying for gold—and when the circumstances are changed, the positions attained, the gold emptied at the feet of the sacrificed heart, they look back and in the despair of their souls cry out:

"'Oh, to have back my liberty! to be released from the maddening sound of my clanking chains! to be free for one human impulse, one throb of my heart's true emotion!' I have had no sympathy, no compassion for those so situated; now I can feel for them. But you, my child, love the being to whom you were united. How happy for you!" and tenderly laying his hand upon her head, he continued, with trembling emotion:

"I loved you when I first saw you, which strange feeling impelled me to attempt your rescue from the watery deep, or die with you there. I loved you more when I watched your unselfish sacrifice toward the suffering of my parish, and, if possible, I love you tenfold more in this moment of anguish in which I know I must lose you."

He could speak no more, he fell on his knees by her side, and the strong man burst into an agony of grief.

"Oh, how shall I bear this sorrow? My cup is overflowing. But why think of myself while you suffer?" And he arose, determined to be stronger than his strongest weakness. "Tell me, my child," as he lovingly stroked her hair; "tell me what you have resolved to do."

Victoria could not reply.

"You cannot think for yourself, let me then advise you: return to your husband, if only to explain his injustice and assert your own innocence; it will relieve your heart and do—something more, if he *ever loved you*."

"Oh, how I wish I could; how I crave to see him once more; but I have not the courage."

"There is One who is able to give you

strength, pray to Him; He will gently lead you."

"I cannot pray! I cannot think! My burden has grown heavier than I can bear."

"Prayer is for the weary, burdened heart," urged the rector.

"'Come unto Me all ye that labor and are heavy laden, and I will give you rest.' Hark! the choir is chanting the same consoling promise. Is it not comforting?"

As the voices floated into the room in the peaceful chant, "Come unto Me," Victoria burst forth in convulsive sobbings.

"If you cannot pray, my dear, I will pray for you," whispered the rector. "Oh, Thou who takest upon Thyself the burdens of Thy children who come to Thee, help Thou this sorrowing one. Worldly consolation avails her no longer. A stronger power must now uphold her. Give her new life to undertake this journey. Protect her, and as she goes from him who loves her with a love as enduring as it is hopeless, bring her safely to her loved one in a distant land, and may we meet in that great Beyond, where all tears are forever wiped away, and parting comes no more."

Dr. Wadsworth's emotion joined the tears of Victoria, and only the echo of the choir floated to their ears an " Amen."

CHAPTER XVII.

THE TRAGIC MEETING.

THE evening of the Roseveer reception had arrived.

Mrs. Rodney was radiant in her noted pearls, and a dress which looked as though it had floated down from angels' wings.

Mr. Rodney slowly entered the drawing-room. His wife looked up quickly, and, noticing his unusual appearance, exclaimed in alarm:

"Why, darling, you are not well!"

He started as though guilty of a crime, but recalling himself, replied lightly:

"I am perfectly well, Nell. Possibly I have smoked too much this evening."

"I think, dear," said Mrs. Rodney, still looking at him, "we had better remain at home. I have a presentiment of evil, and I know you are not well."

"Your 'presentiment' comes from the fact

of Deluth's expected attendance to-night; that should not trouble you," as he proceeded to wrap her in the swans'down cloak she had just thrown aside.

A moment later they had entered their carriage and were off for the Roseveers'.

It was a heavenly night; one by which lovers could see to paint their bliss in each other's eyes, and with Cupid's pencil sketch their future paradise.

The bright moon sailed across the heavens, shedding such a volume of pure light that every object was as distinctly visible as by the clearest midday sun.

Deluth was more than fashionably late. He invariably made a point of being the last, thereby, as he believed, causing the greater sensation.

As his sumptuous apartments were just over the way, he skipped across the street just as a tall figure, with saddened aspect, was nearly in front of the blazing mansion. Hoping the man had not noticed him, Deluth suddenly lowered his hat to his very eyes and quickened his pace.

The next instant the aggrieved and the aggressor stood face to face.

The moon, which had been obscured by a fleeting cloud, electrically shot forth, casting its penetrating rays on the white visage of Charles Déluth.

With a hoarse, breathing sound, Jack Lennox drew back; his face assumed an expression terrible to behold; his eyes looked like balls of fire which must leap forth and consume the guilty antagonist, and, quivering from head to foot with suppressed fury, he was for a moment unable to speak.

The situation was truly an awful one for these two former friends.

In striking contrast with the violent passions which surged within the bosoms of the husband and betrayer was the calm loveliness of the night. Not a breath of wind which seemed equal to sway a drooping lily disturbed the quiet of the scene.

The moon was happy in its unwonted effulgence; it was so bright that every flaw in the pavement, every pebble in the street was distinguishable in the diamond glitter of that silvery light.

Jack Lennox broke the silence as he uttered, in a hollow voice:

"I have cauhgt you at last, Charles Deluth! At last my hour is come!"

Deluth, who by this time had regained all his habitual composure, contemptuously shrugged his shoulders, and replied, with a sneer:

"This is truly dramatic, Mr. Lennox. I can make some allowance for the humiliating *rôle* of a betrayed husband——"

"*Silence!*" thundered forth Lennox. "How dare you add insult to the irreparable injury you have done me! Have you no atom of feeling when you think of the pure woman you have ruined? of me, the friend, you have betrayed, dishonored, robbed?

"You have shattered my life, killed my love; but now we are face to face, and your life shall pay the forfeit!"

As Jack Lennox raised his hand, his opponent stepped back and avoided the tremendous blow.

"Fool!" hissed Deluth, "you had better not tempt me too far. I am not to be trifled with."

"Nor am I," hoarsely whispered Lennox. "I am reduced to boyish weakness through my long suffering, but you shall not escape me! I will stop your devilish career, and prevent you from making other victims."

He could say no more. His dry breath scorched his very lips, but his ashen face and dilating eyes, which seemed starting from their sockets, caused even the hardened Deluth to recoil.

Quickly recovering himself, however, he permitted only a fiendish sneer to escape him.

A moment more and Jack Lennox, though physically weak, held Deluth in a grasp of iron.

The life and death struggle seemed to check the progress of the calmly-sailing moon, while the pitying stars looked down in tearful sympathy with the heartbroken husband.

Outraged honor was fast gaining the ascendancy, as the two men fell on the pavement, frantically struggling.

At last Deluth put forth all his strength, dragged himself from beneath his adversary, and reaching back drew from his pocket a pistol.

A flash, a groan, and Jack Lennox fell back, bleeding.

Deluth hesitated what to do, but finally decided to brush the soil from his outside coat, which he removed, and, arranging his disordered dress, ascended to the Roseveer mansion, while muttering to himself:

"Fool! he brought it on himself. I warned him. Why did he tempt me?" and then calmly entered the blaze of perfumed lights.

After greeting the hostess, his friends noticed that he was somewhat pale, and one of them, scanning him through his glasses, remarked:

"What the deuce is the matter with you, Deluth? You look as though you had seen a ghost. You are positively ill."

"Oh, nothing," replied Deluth, trying to

look cheerful. "Damp air, or something. I feel a little chilly."

Clang! clang! clang! fiercely went the door-gong.

A policeman entered, and excitedly asked:

"Can anyone present identify the body of a gentleman who has just been shot in front of this house?"

A footman ran down the steps, and at once recognized in the prostrate form, Mr. Lennox, his former employer.

He sprang up the steps into the parlor, and breathlessly whispered to Mr. Rodney:

"Come—Mr. Lennox!"

Mr. Rodney, who had just caught sight of Deluth, and, with pale face, was going toward him, hurriedly followed the servant to the pavement.

One look, and he raised the deathlike body, instinctively knowing all.

"Can you speak? One word to identify the villain who has attempted your life.

"Make an effort! Strive to understand me!

"If Deluth is the assassin, give me one look!"

As a specter might gaze, even so mechanically opened, for one brief instant, the eyes of Jack Lennox, and darted a gleam of acknowledgment.

Leaving the wounded man with the servant, Rodney motioned the police to follow, and quickly re-entered the drawing-room.

Deluth was the center of an admiring throng.

Ladies rudely jostled each other vying for a first congratulatory welcome to the darling of society.

As music announced dancing, the hostess was in the act of accepting the arm of her honored (?) guest, when Rodney's voice thrilled with horror everyone present.

"Officers, arrest that cowardly murderer, Charles Deluth, double assassin of Jack Lennox!"

Deluth was placed under arrest and was walking down the steps with the officers, when a strange looking figure sprang near him, glared and chuckled.

"Ha! ha! they've got you! Soon I'll have you! I'll have you yet!" and away he bounded with the swiftness of a deer.

Poor Will Darrow was seeking to avenge his sister Bess, and had mistaken the strong resemblance of Deluth for the person of John Walton.

CHAPTER XVIII.

UNFORGIVING.

THE examination of Deluth proved all his dearest admirers could desire. Even women gained admittance to the witness room, peered and listened through doors, while others, heavily veiled, were seated in the court room, "so sorry" were they for "dear Mr. Deluth," and anxious that no harm come to the profligate millionaire.

Upon the verdict of "self-defense," men flocked around him, and even his fair friends forgot that they desired to remain *incognito*, and flinging back their veils rushed upon the scapegrace, congratulating the Mephistopheles of their adoration.

Jack Lennox was removed to his Cousin Ned's house, where for weeks life and death swayed in the balance, casting a gloom over everyone.

Even the faint sweep of Melpomene, as she passed through in her sad vigils, seemed to jar on the deathlike silence which pervaded the Rodney home, until, to the intense happiness of his friends, Jack Lennox recovered, and was daily seen out driving.

The light, warm, cheerful room was in strong contrast to the dark, windy night, thunder and lightning striving for supremacy. Suddenly a piteous moan echoed through the house.

Mr. Rodney turned pale at the sound of that voice, and, rushing into the hall, he saw the form of Jack Lennox's wife, poor Victoria, supported in the arms of Joe Jungle.

A moment more and he laid her on a sofa in the library, while Nell Rodney, with streaming eyes, was endeavoring to revive the wreck of her once dearest friend, now lying unconscious before her.

A physician was summoned, and after hours of patient labor the unhappy woman opened her eyes, but reason was gone.

The fearful strain upon her already shattered health was too much for her strength, and a sight of the Rodney home had recalled more than her weakened brain could bear. She now fell into mutterings, as she imagined herself in the ball-room with Deluth.

"Promise? My 'word'? Yes; well then I will redeem my word, but this shall be my last waltz.

"Ah! The music!

"Inspiring music!

"Heavenly music!

"I am waltzing to the music!

"He smiles!

"I fear him!

"He presses me to his throbbing breast!

"My heart quickens!

"My brain reels!

"My head falls on his bosom!

"His hot breath burns my cheek!

"He whispers! Whispers!

"We float in air! In air!

"Waltzing—waltzing to music!"

Her voice died away in imaginings of the past, then, suddenly, rang out in horror—

"Ah! That waltz has killed his love—my life!

"Husband, forgive—forgive!"

Anguished Joe Jungle raised the fragile Victoria in his trembling arms, when, from a shuddering, wild look, her face lighted into radiance, her lips moved, "Father," and she fell asleep, like a wearied child, in the arms of her adopted parent.

The next day Victoria Lennox awakened in a room which little she imagined was under the same roof with that of her heart-broken husband.

Her faithful, loving friend was beside her in a moment.

Poor Victoria's memory, though not quite right, was sufficiently so to recognize the home of the Rodneys.

The tears trickled down her quivering face as she asked: "I here? Ah, Nell, how different to the spurnings of everyone from whom I sought information. Tell me, is Jack alive and well?" and she burst into sobbings.

Nell Rodney knew how futile had been the

urgings for Jack Lennox to see his wife ever since her arrival, and dared not inform Victoria of his presence in the house; she therefore answered her questions as kindly as possible.

"My mind is not very clear," said the desolate wife, as she pressed her thin hands to her burning temples; "but I remember going to Mrs. Vaintone's the day I arrived from Europe, to beg news of Jack—that was all; but she sneered at my misery, as others had done.

"Then for the second time I sought that irresistible death which beckons those who abandon hope; that mysterious companion who follows every step of the conscientious who blights the life of those they love.

"Over flowers and through thorns, there stands the reaper, with grim visage and mocking laugh, pointing to his scythe, while demanding, 'Your life! your life! the interest of your sin!'

"Ah, Nell, how glad I am to go, if only I could see him, my loved husband, once more," and an avalanche of tears streamed down her white cheeks, which seemed equal to melt the remnant of her despairing heart.

"Oh, if I had not been frightened into fleeing, after that deadly waltz, which has caused all this sorrow. I was innocent of one wrong thought. I am innocent of a wrong act to my husband; but like all others, he believes me guilty."

"No, no," replied Nell Rodney; "you must not say that. All did not lose faith in you. Aunt Sophronie, Ned and I knew you were incapable of willful wrong. Your flight was the unpardonable and mysterious part to those who believed in you; yet I knew even that mad act would eventually be shown as the diabolical plan of another.

"But we will speak no more of this now, simply hope that all will——"

"Ah! Do not give me hope," interrupted Victoria; "let my heart remain in its dark, deep pool of despair.

"It will soon be over; the best physicians have given me but three months to live. Ah, what happiness that is to me; so soon to lay down my weary burden and find rest in heaven. How sweet the promise, 'And I will give you rest'! If only I could see Jack, just to whisper, 'I am innocent;'" and tears again rained down her pale cheeks.

Nell Rodney forced herself to laugh and be merry. "Well, Vic, dear, you are not strong enough to carve a marble Hercules, or sketch a centennial parade for a morning newspaper; but you are in no such danger as your comforting physicians have led you to believe. I suppose they asked a heavy fee in consideration of the extra nail they drove in your last architectural habitation. Have you any of their medicines? If so, I will throw them out. You shall be taken out of that bed, be dressed, and have a drive with me after I return from shopping. While Aunt Sophronie and I are away, you can run all over the house, take a good look in all the rooms, and tell me how to alter them according to your usual artistic ideas."

"She'll be sure to meet Jack," thought Mrs. Rodney.

"Your palatial little home is just as you left it," added Aunt Sophronie, as she kissed Vic and went on talking as coolly as though she did not ache to press her beloved niece to her heart and have a real good sympathy-crying duet.

She never forgot how she had urged Victoria, against her will, to attend that fateful reception one year before, and one of her strongest arguments in favor of the wife of Jack Lennox had been the persistent desire of Vic to remain at home, in the fond anticipation that her husband might return that night and she would be there to receive him.

After hearing Joe Jungle's story, and, with the others, appealed to Jack and reasoned with him to no avail, her patience took to its wings, and left her in a woefully fluttering, spluttering frame of mind.

"I won't put up with this state of affairs very long without telling Jack Lennox what I think of him. One would suppose no one suffered through this but himself, and that we must all stroke him down, pat him, weep over him, and repeat 'Poor Jack!' sixty times an hour, to our tear-dripping handkerchiefs.

"Jack Lennox is unfeeling, and, like most men, stubborn as a mule—worse; for, after a mule has had its own will, kicked, reared, plunged, and pitched, it will settle down to common sense, take up the bit and go on its way rejoicing as if nothing had occurred to make it balky.

"But a man—oh, defend me from a man when he has an attack of sulkiness; he's a burial in the country, with the mourners standing two feet deep in sleeting snow, waiting for the town grave-digger to finish the legal depth.

"Then, talk about 'inflexible old maids' long faces;' why, in comparison to such men, we're the condensed fun of a thousand youngsters bursting their sides at a Punch and Judy pantomime.

"I know now Vic was always too good for him, maybe he abused her. Anyway, he hasn't shown a particle of feeling since she entered this house. And he's 'going to China,' is he? Let him go! I'll disinherit him, and give every penny of his share to Vic's adopted father, and we'll all go to housekeeping and just show Jack Lennox that we can manage to breathe, and be happy, too, without him.

"Mr. Jungle is the most sensible man I ever spoke with; he suits me better than all the college-bred men, whose insipid attentions I've been bored with all my life—yes, yes, I'm coming," as she was aroused from her reverie by a call from Nell that she was going to her dressmaker's, and would return for her in a few moments. "Well," said she, "we won't be gone long, Vic, and you just kind of roam through the house, and if you should find another man roaming—I mean if you should see a man anywhere in the house—oh, don't look so frightened, not a burglar—but—well, you know—Ned is having the sidewalk fixed, and a man might come in the kitchen for a glass of water, and in case he should miss his way, and find himself upstairs in any of the rooms, why you'll know he belongs there—I mean —don't be frightened, you'll know he's only a man, and just look at him as if you didn't know him, and didn't wish to know him."

Aunt Sophronie kept getting into deeper water, and fled just in time to meet Joe Jungle at the door, who desired to speak with her concerning Victoria, whereupon, to avoid interruption, they adjourned to Mrs. Rodney's sitting-room. By way of introduction, Mr. Jungle said to Miss Rodney:

"I see ye didn't go ter church yes'day; don't you 'tend meetin'?"

"I have not for many years," replied Miss Rodney. "I found there were hypocrites in the church; one man particularly, who married a friend of mine about that time, but they never lived happily, so it paid him up for breaking—" and Miss Rodney coughed, as she felt she had said too much.

"Why, you're too sensible to blame the church fur hypocrites," replied Mr. Jungle. "The best parrents have had some of the wo'st and the finest children all brought up under the same influence. Ef we go to blamin' churches fur disgraceful hypocrites, we ken go through all the best institutions of the civilized world an' knock um all deown on the same principle, fur they all 'casionally get stuck with bad people. You'd better look eout. When you help inferdelity by stayin' away from the meetin'-heouse you're helpin' them that fust attacks churches, then other good institutions, an' finish up by a' outburst 'gainst all law, all order, all forms of gov'ment, till they become a howlin' mob of anarchists.

"When eour barbarous war wuz over, some didn't like to have thar salaries stopped, ached fur more excitement, an' where they stood a good chance of gettin' top the heap in suthin' new; so some rushed off to Russia an' fanned that deadly fire uv anarchy, others flew to Ireland with their big idle bellows, which they pumped till they got a red-hot flame started in that touch-and-go-off country. Wongersoll tried stayin' at home, but gettin' tired of dry, slow law, concluded to start a kind o' religi's circus, where he knew he could be first clown an' rake in all the money. Uv course some folks would go, expectin' to hear a kind o' lectur', but they never heard nothin' more'n I did—Wongersoll sayin's and Bible jokes interduced into a circus ring.

"Then this wonderful inferdel took pride in havin' his daughters boast to press reporters, for publication, that they never 'entered a church' er 'prayed a prayer in thar lives.' I kent see whar the wonderful lesson of morality comes in thar, fur sence the fust proof-sheets of history was read by the inhabitants uv this world, I never heard uv a man er woman concoctin' any devilment while they war communin' with thar Maker. Then to fu'ther advertise his electrotyped-joke-trade, he boasts his father was a clergyman; that's sad fur the parrents, but there air freaks uv hostile, ungrateful children in these days as well as in the days uv Mrs. Nero's son and Mr. Lear's daughter Goneril.

"Wongersoll's coarse ridicule an' vulgar jokes haz done more to crush out the good influence of parrents' teachin' than all the other vices of the nineteenth century.

He's gittin' kind o' 'shamed o' inferdelity neow, an' his latest billhead reads 'Scientific Religion.' That's another way uv gittin' 'reound to wipe eout a Supreme Being. Neow ef some astronomer that wuz out uv a job would come 'reound an' say:

" 'Come on, Wongersoll, big money; I'm a scientist—way up in sun, moon an' stars, an' that kind o' thing; ain't busy neow; s'posin' we rig up a' Edison phonograph, an' I'll sail away in a b'loon to heaven an' take deown the sayin's of th' Almighty from Himself direct. I'll say you sent me, an' ef He don't give me a' audience you'll tell jokes abeout Him and talk 'gainst His very existence.' Neow ef that could be done Wongersoll would 'plaud an' say, 'See, that's scientific religion, cause a' astronomer understands it all, and then I hold all the stock uv the new sensation— dollar a head.'

"But no 'stronomer ever yet got audience with the Almighty, not even the great English scientist Glashier, who had the equally great b'loonist to take him up seven miles inter unknown space, till they both most died uv breathin' pure air, but lived to come back an' tell us jess as little as a baby shakin' a tin rattle-box in eour ears. No 'stronomer ever penetrated the designs er the domains uv the Almighty until He took um from earth fur good, an' none uv 'em ever come back to give us lessons in scientific religion, er to tell wonderful, mortal man heow to compete with his Maker's own patent in perducing human life, or resuscitatin' the dead after that life was called in by its Patentee.

"If inferdels an' anarchists—they're both alike—had their way to-day, had overthrown churches an' gov'ments, uprooted all law, all order, the very fust thing they'd start in on would be to go fightin' among themselves fur the very same positions uv kings, queens, presidents and land owners, that they'd jest bombarded, an' when the majority won, the others would find themselves jess where they air neow, on'y worse, fur they'd have a load of dissatisfaction to carry in their hearts that the law-abidin' man, who honestly earns his livin', don't feel neow in his contented mind, which is away ahead of the millionaire's ceaseless worry. Anyone knows one heour brain work is worse than twenty-four heours uv physical labor.

"Neow, as I was sayin' about the uprootin' business, if Wongersoll didn't get his political pull then tew, he'd be the fust one to light on to startin' a church, climb into the pulpit, an' say to the same audiences he's had in inferdelity, 'I'm here to tell you you're a common, vulgar set o' brutes not to acknowledge your Maker; don't ye know all decent humanity du that? Neow you ken come an' hear me tell abeout it, dollar a head; law is ruther dry an' slow jes neow, an' this thing's got to pay.'

"Jest notice, Miss Rodney, you don't find no Protestant missionaries exilin' themselves to sufferin', hunger and death, strivin' to benefit humanity; no Roman Catholic Father Damiens to give their lives to the lepers; no saintly sisters uv charity uv all creeds who consecrate their worldly existence to doin' good. Ye don't find no sech characters 'mong inferdels er arnichists of any country. Their cry instead is 'land!' 'gold!' which they never earned, er was willed to um. An' like the highwayman grabs the throat of the fust man he dares attack, an' says, 'The world owes me a livin' in my own way, an' I'm goin' to have it, or its life. Give up your gold— your gold!'

"Inferdelity is the cradle of a smoldering rebellion to-day, which is surely eatin' into the core of every gov'ment in the civilized world. The unsuspicious, law abidin' considers it but hot-headed child's play; we go to sleep in imagined peace and security, when, lo! the headsmen Inferdelity, Anarchy and Rebellion air at our bedside, and we are lost!"

If Aunt Sophronie had before been taken with Joe Jungle, she was now completely captivated with his sound reasoning and unexpected eloquence, but as she did not wish to give in at once, returned to the church subject.

"Well, Mr. Jungle, while I think you are perfectly correct in what you have expressed, still, you must admit the church at large is not what it ought to be, and in past ages its members have been guilty of that which——"

"Wongersoll ag'in!" interrupted Joe Jungle. "Pardon me, Miss Rodney, ef I say don't give me such weak stuff-argument ez that feller frosts his stale cakes with. No one is silly 'nough to deny that fur highest morality, ef nothin' else, the church is the best institution the world has ever had. It ain't infallible, 'cause it takes in all kinds, tryin' to make um better; an' its mistakes don't wipe eout the Almighty who made us, er curse the church fur individual crimes.

"When fathers, sons an' brothers murdered each other to the funeral dirges of two million uv eour best men, that didn't wipe eout eour gov'ment, er say that Abraham Lincoln was a dastard. Didn't the United States gov'ment live through it all, an' stands firmer to-day than ever, some uv its staunchest supporters bein' the very men who attempted its life? Do ye think ef we'd had the experience of the most barbarous war that ever disgraced a civilized people, we'd resorted to murder, to argue and right that which should with all nations be referred to a World's Conference for settlement? But ye don't catch us at it ag'in; we know better neow, an' will be the fust civilized country to set the long needed example of abolishing legal murder.

"An all-wise Being, who has ever withheld from us the secret of givin' er restorin' human life, has never acceded to mortal man the right to take that life under the plea uv *legal* killin.'

"That awful sentence of banishment, 'Siberia!' deals a thousand more dreaded blows than the glistenin' axe of the executioner.

"When the calm judgment of a' enlightened gov'ment kent rise above a' insane er depraved murderer in dealin' with bloody crimes; that gov'ment sheould hide its head in the oblivion uv the fu'thest corner of the dark ages, nor dare look in the face a civilized, God-forgiv'n humanity.

"The church, the meetin'-house uv eour Creator's school childurn, has profited by experience tu; it needs cleansin' an' purifyin' neow, an' ef it don't go to work whitewashin' an' scrubbin', and git cleaned up, infectious diseases will seize hold on't that'll take time, trouble an' sorrow to 'radicate."

"Mrs. Rodney, ma'am, is at the door in the coupé waitin' fur ye ma'am," interrupted a servant.

"'Scuse me keepin' ye, we'll talk 'beout Victoria when you return; meanwhile I'm goin' to interview that man Lennix," said Jungle, as he slyly took Miss Rodney's hand, which gentle pressure recalled to her the hypocrite sweetheart who married the other girl. Was that why she blushed, stammered and rushed away, making the quickest shopping expedition of her life? or did the smile of a big, honest heart effectually blind her vision to beautiful dry goods? What a recipe for some husband's weeping check-books, did they understand how little it really takes to make a good woman happy.

Victoria could not realize why her aunt should suppose she would be timid in the home of Nell Rodney. "Oh," reasoned she, "they think because I have been ill, that I am dangerously nervous. I will go over the dear house just to show how strong I am: and that my nerves are not weak;" to prove which she immediately went into hysterics, thinking of her husband, and clasping her hands, she exclaimed: "Oh, if only I had Jack, how happy I would be! Jack! Jack! my Jack!"

Roby and Ruby had entered the room without Victoria's knowledge, and the two little dears now fled to the nursery for consultation what was best to do for "Auntie Lennox." Roby proposed showing her his zebra, woolly horse, steam-engine, fire-ladders and numerous other wonderful inventions which he thought must please her.

Ruby smiled upon him with such a patronizing air that he dropped everything and finally bullied her as to her superior knowledge, saying with conscious pride:

"Youm no older'n me, an I'm a man. What do Auntie Wennox want, den? You know so much 'bout ev'thing."

Ruby straightened herself and haughtily replied, with the instinct of her sex: "Well, Auntie don't want a woolly hoss or a steam-engine when her was cwyin' for Jack. 'My Jack,' her said."

A brilliant idea seemed to shoot into Roby's cranium as he darted away, repeating to himself, "I know! I know!"

Ruby followed, but she only caught sight of his heels, and she muttered, "Brover will break him's neck, I guess," and then dignifiedly strode after him.

CHAPTER XIX.

RUBY'S INSTINCT.

> "Ah well! for us all some sweet hope lies
> Deeply buried from human eyes;
> And in the hereafter, angels
> May roll the stone from its grave away."
> —*Whittier.*

JACK LENNOX was packing some few books in the library, to take with him on a voyage to China, from which destination he emphatically stated he would "never return."

Carelessly he opened a volume of Whittier's poems, when his eyes fell upon the lines:

> "God pity them both, and pity us all,
> Who vainly the dreams of youth recall;
> For of all sad words of tongue or pen,
> The saddest are, 'It might have been.'"

Amidst his agonizing thoughts, a domestic appeared and handed a large card, largely written, with a large amount of information, which read:

> *Joseph Jungle*
> *a American*
> *Jungle*
> *Jungle County*
> *Arizona terittorray*
> *united states of America*
> *U S A*

The servant strove to conjure up awful visions of being discharged, and finally, after getting ready a handkerchief to protect a twitching facial play, looked down and measuredly delivered the message: "The gentleman told me, sir—to tell you—sir—to *turn over!*"

Such a pleasant impulse as a smile had long been a stranger to the heartbroken husband. He was about to return the card when his eye caught something written on its reverse side, which caused him to grow pale with anger, as he read:

Sir ez i'm the dopted father of your wife Miss Victoria Lennox Jungle i would Perciate a interview beout my Dawter ef you re a Man an Aint tew sick

J Jungle

Jack Lennox walked across the room as though he were measuring it by yard strides for a new carpet, then turning to the domestic, madly gasped, "Show'm in!"

Joe Jungle was no sooner in the library than the husband began:

"I suppose you are here to ask for certain moneys legally belonging, as support, to—a person bearing my name; who has, no doubt, squandered more than her private income, the principal of which is beyond her control.

"I will make my allowance ample for her reasonable *personal* support,"—and he gave a meaning look, indicating he did not propose to provide for vagabond adopted fathers—"and will fix the amount at $5,000 per annum.

"The arrangement for payment may be found at my lawyers, Messrs. Henry C.

Andrews & Co.," and Mr. Lennox resumed the packing of his books.

Joe Jungle about this time looked a little savage also, but quickly solved his plan.

"The fust thing," thought he, "I'll sit deown. I s'pose it ain't perlite in York to ask a man to take a cheir, 'cause it might look like a reflection on his intulligence that he don't know 'nuff ter sit deown hisself witheout bein' invited. No wonder I git all mixed up on etiquit the way everything's changin'.

"When I wuz a boy a feller wouldn't be asked to a corn huskin' bee that hed sich perliteness ez that; but I guess Washingtonian manners air good 'nuff fur me yet awhile, en I notice one thing, the perlitest people I ever hed dealin's with, was them that showed their perliteness through a kind heart to thar fellar bein'." And he seated himself comfortably in a chair as he began:

"Wall, 'beout the money, Mr. Lennix, mebbe 'twould be a good thing; she may need it. I've heard o' women who didn't know when to stop tradin' at stores, an' she may hev spent her last dollar. She ain't much on trinkets, but her sickness may hev turned her head since she arrived forty-eight heour ago on the steamer.

"Yes'day was Sunday, an' I didn't know she'd been eout ter-day lookin' 'reound; but she may've been, an' stopped on her way an' bought eout Tiffany an' a few dry goods stores—jess to du a little shoppin', and so used up her fourteen million that she hed day 'fore yes'day in her eown right; an' p'r'aps neow she's sufferin' fur a leetle change; she might 'perciate the change—ef it was connected with you—but I ain't here to tell kernundrums."

Jack Lennox could not understand how Ned Rodney tolerated this Wayback to such familiarity as he had shown him for the last two days, and additionally thought that the vagabond was touched in the head, talking about his "adopted daughter and her fourteen millions," and had decided to quickly end the interview when Joe Jungle burst forth anew:

"Ez I wuz sayin', I didn't come here to git off kernundrums, but to ask you, ez my 'dopted son-in-law, what you intend deoin'?"

Lennox looked aghast, and glaringly replied: "Confine your relationship to other quarters. As to myself, I shall not be intruded upon again, as I leave to-morrow for China."

"Nothin' like a sea ride fur gineral health. I was awfully bilious 'fore I started from London, but I made a gin'rous conterbution to th' Atlantic Ocean, an' got rid o' all my bile an' dyspepsy stock at onct, an' I don't b'lieve I'll have ter take a dose uv med'cine in six months. China's a good way off— good way," said Jungle, in a softened voice. "An' ye ain't goin' ter leave without seein' that brokenhearted leetle girl upsta'rs that loves ye, be ye?"

Jack Lennox viciously hissed: "If you came here to insult me, and think I will bear it patiently, you are mistaken. Were it not that you are a much older man than I, you would before this have been thrown out of that window!"

"Whew!" whistled Joe Jungle. "Wall,

talkin' 'beout age, I guess I ain't eny older'n you be! I'll bet ye! Git eout yer family ricord! An' ez fur throwin' me out that window, du you think I'd be drinkin' milk while ye war doin' it? Now you'd better cool deown and let us talk common sense.

"I kneow it's been purty hard on you, an 'twas an awful mistake to fly t'Europe instead uv waitin' to pertest her innercence, after you heard that villian talk to her in the conservatory; 'pearances was awfully 'g'inst her, but she w'an't guilty then, an' she's never been guilty sence of a wrong act er thought.

"She wuz crazy when you swooned at her feet, an' then that villian hustled her away onter a steamer by tellin' her you'd 'never furgive her,' fur you 'b'lieved her guilty' an' would kill 'both on um at sight.'

"Twa'n't till arter the steamer was eout ter sea that she realized what she'd done an' the villiany of D'luth, an' then she jumped inter th' ocean ter 'scape him fu'ther. A parson jumped in arter her an' saved her ter live an' clear herself 'fore you an' the world; an' now she's here under my pertection, an' she'll du it!

"Ye see, I wuz on the ship with her when it burned up, an' my on'y child—my boy—leetle Hank," and Jungle's eyes filled with tears, "wuz burned to death thar. Your wife wuz the on'y woman that laid him eout an' teched his leetle face 'fore he wuz buried at sea. I wuz a' inferdel 'fore then, but that made me know better, an' arter I got ter London I kept goin' with the same parson who saved Victoria's life.

"She went ter church thar tew, so we kept up the 'quaintance. The parson thought a heap on her, an' wanted ter marry her, s'posed she wuz a widder, ye kneow, but she teold him she loved the man she married, an' she would never love er marry 'nother. She spent her time in doin' good an' makin' statues out o' mud—clay—an' heow she did work. That wuz a good thing; people who work never git in mischief, an' it took her thoughts from her sorrow.

"I wa'n't eddicated, but she was, an' I thought she wuz a widder tew, an' I hed no one ter tell me what ter du with fourteen million uv trublomsome money, ner no one ter leave it tew, so I was jess goin' ter perpose to her the day she told me she'd refused the parson.

"I knowed ef she'd refused that splendid man, she wouldn't think uv me, an' the poor child looked so desolate lonesum, I asked her to be my 'dopted dawter, so I could turn over my money to her and pertect her. I hed the papers all made eout, turned over my fourteen million to her, an' become her own father the next day."

"This is nothing to me," haughtily responded Lennox, "beyond the fact that you may be honest, but for the others, I will not hear any gotten up story by either of them to add insult to the irreparable injury wrought me—my deathblow!"

"I know it's purty hard ter b'lieve, but ef Victoray hed on'y told me all 'beout it, heow she'd continued ter ask that fiend ter write you, exoneratin' her in ever' way, he'd o' done it, ez sure ez my name's Joseph Jungle; but he's here in York neow, an' he'll have ter du it yet.

"Ye see, Victoray never went nowhar with him, an' treated him like a stranger, an' it made him so mad, the on'y revenge was in knowin' you b'lieved her guilty."

Despite himself, Jack Lennox was listening to what he termed "exasperating stuff." "I would not," said he, "believe in that woman's innocence if she were dead and I saw my name carved upon her heart! Speak no more to me, I cannot bear it!"

"I kneow it's purty hard, an' ter think that all this misery come through waltzin', an' ye know she wa'n't ter blame fur doin' huggin' dances, when she come up that way. Pity sech a nice woman couldn't been brought up deeferent. Why, my Jinnie wouldn't waltz with anyone she wa'n't related tew. She called it 'huggin' to music'; she said 'thar wuz plenty respectable dances that she could injoy more'n them that let sev'ral men hug a woman 'reound a ball-room.' Th' other women made fun on her, an' said awful vicious things 'beout her for it; but she didn't take no notice on't.

"I was awful 'stonished when I feound sich a nice modest lady ez Victoray waltzed; er that such manners hed got ter be tolerated among eddicated people, even church folks.

"Wall, de ye know that night uv the ball she'd told D'luth that she would never waltz ag'in 'cause her husband, that was yeou, she thought, didn't like it. Finally D'luth told her she hed 'ready promised tew waltz with him, an' when he wouldn't give up, she said 'jess ter keep her word she would, but that would be th' last time she'd ever waltz ag'in in the world fureveran'——"

"Say no more! I know the finish—I was there!" and Jack Lennox heaved a sigh and closed his eyes as though he would shut out the remembrance of that awful scene and his consequent sufferings.

"I know its purty hard, but even ef she was guilty, you might furgive her; but when she ain't, an' you've nothin' to furgive, I ken't see how ye refuse ter fergive her. Ef yeou war in her place an' not been innercent, but really been guilty, wouldn't she furgive yeou?"

"That makes no difference," burst from Jack Lennox; "I am a man!"

"An' ye mean a man ken du anything, even the wo'st kind, an' all must be swallered by the woman; but ef a moth gits in a man's wardrobe, er his wife wuz born with a mole on her neck, that don't jump off with his fust kiss, he thinks it's a reflection on what he calls his 'manhood,' and treats her accordin'ly." Joe Jungle sprang to his feet and jammed both hands in his pockets.

"Jess makes me foamin' mad ter hear men talk 'beout a woman as 'a weaker vessel,' till some disaster comes 'long, then they expect her, like Galati', ter suddenly become a livin' bein', hev 'xperi'nce and big brain all in a minnit; manage the ship, captain an' crew, an' see the cargo safely inter harbor with all odds ag'in her, that would put the biggest, blusterin' six-foot man right under water. Jess makes me foamin'!"

At this point a commotion in the hall was heard, and the footman darted in saying: "Mr. Deluth—just been stabbed down the street by that crazy Will Darrow. Mr. Deluth thinks he's dying, and was brought here to see Mr. Lennox."

Before Jack Lennox could prevent it, two men appeared supporting the form of Charles Deluth, whose glassy eyes told that he had but a few moments to live. He gasped:

"Your wife is innocent—pure as when—you last held her—in your arms—I am guilty—dying—will you forgive? Oh, forgive!"

Then his eyes roamed to Joe Jungle.

"My life has been wrong—I never thought of it—until you spoke to me of death—that time—I thought—I would never die! Oh! for one week of life—one day—one hour! Ah!" and he clutched at his neck as though choking.

Once more Deluth begged the wronged

husband to speak the one word 'forgiveness'; but he might as well have appealed to adamant.

Jack Lennox motioned the men to take away their helpless charge, while no fiber of the husband's frame stirred with human feeling, other than that of implacable hatred, which darted from his glaring eyes in answer to the appeals of his dying enemy.

The latter was taken to his carriage, and thence to the house from whence he and his profligate companions had emerged one hour before; and there, in a gilded palace of sin, amid wild revelry, he died with his last fading, agonizing vision resting on the besotted and dissolute of both sexes, whose companionship had been for Charles Deluth, highest ambition, happiness paramount. Fitting close to such careers as his.

As the lunatic, Will Darrow, struck Deluth's deathblow a flash of reason showed him he had mistaken his victim for that of John Walton, and away he darted with gleaming eyes, still chuckling, "I'll have him yet! I'll have him yet!"

Jack Lennox sat down as stolidly as though nothing unusual had occurred. At last Joe Jungle broke the oppressive silence.

"Mr. Lennox, you've jess heard from a dyin' man that your wife is a' innocent woman. Don't ye want ter see her? She ain't got long ter live. She's been purty bad, an' the doctor says she's dyin' uv a broken heart. Ag'in, she's never got over that awful plunge in the Atlantic a year ago. She's got heart disease neow."

Jack Lennox had just separated his lips to order the man from his presence who could presume to stab him with appeals for sympathy for her who had disgraced him and blighted his life, when he was silenced by the entrance of Roby, who rushed to his uncle, carrying a large rabbit, and with trembling lips confided his sorrow.

"Uncle Wennox, Auntie Wennox was cwyin' hard, an' callin' for Jack,—'Oh, give me my Jack!' her said. Then I runned and got my jack-rabbit for her; but her wou'n' rook at him, an' I don't know what to give her," and Roby burst forth in stifled sobs.

Ruby walked sorrowfully in just as Roby gave fresh vent to tears, and asked, "What Jack can I give her now, Uncle Jack?"

Ruby's womanly instinct was again inspired as she innocently looked up into Jack Lennox's face.

"Uncu Jack, youm name is Jack! Guess youms be the Jack she wants. I see if—I see if—" and away she ran, followed by Roby, whose jack-rabbit lost no time on the homestretch for his preferred quarters in the garden.

Joe Jungle cleared his throat several times, and was now inspecting the ceiling ornamentation; but what a picture was Jack Lennox! The conflicting emotions which betrayed themselves in the man's quivering frame and blanched features was a tragic study; the alternation of tenderest love and deepest hatred, making a light and shadow on his face no Rembrandt hand could paint.

Victoria had recovered from her violent hysteria, and was following Nell's injunction to look in all the rooms, with a view to assisting her at refurnishing, etc. She had wandered through a portion of the upper part of the house, and was now on her way to inspect the library.

All was so quiet, she thought she was in no danger of meeting anyone, so vacantly glided in, and raising her eyes to a marble bust of her own carving, saw no one until she struck against a chair, at which a man sprung up. Victoria gasped, "Jack!" and fell in the arms of her trembling husband.

How can pen picture the pity, the forgiveness exchanged in that one moment of indescribable anguish and happiness.

Poor Victoria! She looked like the frayed cord of hope, which, having reached its longings, must snap at the weight of its own breath.

Pitying angels stood guard, while the low, convulsive sobs of husband and wife appealed to high heaven for sympathy and pardon.

Joe Jungle was overcome at the picture before him, and quietly stole out.

"Ah," whispered Victoria, with a thrill of

delight as she felt the arms of her husband around her, "how kind of Heaven to grant me my last prayer. I do not deserve this great happiness. Death is welcome now."

"My love," said Jack Lennox, and his body shook with suppressed agony, "do not speak of death. Live! live! We will again be happy."

He raised her wan, sweet face, while her dark, loving eyes shone like glittering diamonds.

As he pressed his arms close about her, she hid her head in his bosom like a frightened child.

"Hold me, darling! Don't let me go! Don't let me be taken from you."

"You shall not die, my love!" hoarsely exclaimed her husband.

"When almost dead from physical suffering," said Victoria, "I began that journey from Europe to gratify the cravings of my hungry heart.

"And now I am here, pillowed on your loving breast, while your gentle arms will bear me, pleadingly, to the throne of heaven."

Jack Lennox moaned an appeal.

"Have pity! oh, have pity! my wife! my love! Do not speak of leaving me! All is forgiven! We are again united! Death alone can part us now!"

And despairing grief burst forth from his long pent-up feelings.

"Oh, darling," whispered his wife, "I have so longed for a sight of your face—I have so hungered for the sound of your voice—I have so prayed for this happy moment—to be held in your loving arms!

"I lived when others thought me dead; dragged myself in imagination to where you slept—crept to your side—held my lips to inhale your loving breath, and drank new life to see this moment!"

It was truly heaven's sunlight which thousand softened hues smiled through the stained glass window, as a halo around the heads of Jack and Victoria Lennox, whose hearts again truly beat as one.

Joe Jungle was happy, and after explaining to Aunt Sophronie, who had returned, added :

"Neow that my 'dopted dawter has found a husband, I'm goin' ter follow her good 'xample, ef I kin git Miss Sophronie Rodney fur the 'dopted father's wife.

"I ain't no long-faced blue law, an' I'm a great sight happier sence I acknowledged my Creator, with whom I commune. I b'lieve He wants us to enjoy ourselves, jess ez we du eour childurn, rational an' right, without goin' tew fur. Neow we ken have a big swell weddin', at some roomy hippodrome, with a dozen bands. What d'ye say?"

"I agree," blushed Aunt Sopronie, "minus the hippodrome."

The twins, who had been looking everywhere for their Auntie, ran by as Mr. Jungle was saying to his *fiancee :* "An' we'll give them twins a million apiece. Ruby, the wise leetle critter, kerries eout what I've allers said 'beout a bright woman, ' thar insteenct is more'n a man ken ever study in books.' She knowed what was lackin' in a minnit, an' showed Jack Lennox what he

Ruby called in a loud whisper: " Come, brover, come! I fink Auntie Wennox hash foun' her Jwack!"
(Page 253.)

didn't b'lieve himself, that he had a heart and loved his wife as much as ever.

"Neow jess take my arm, an' I'll interduce ye to my dawter and son-in-law," and away they strode, a handsome couple; for though their hair was streaked with white, their hearts were pink blossoms, blushing in the warm sunshine of human happiness.

The presentation had taken place when Ruby's voice was heard in a very loud whisper from where she was peeking in at the scene.

"Come, brover, come! I fink Auntie Wennox hash foun' her Jack."

While laughing waves of joy break into the haven of rest, two women are being rightfully *hugged to music*, Nell Rodney softly playing, "I Gathered Shells in Days Before."

> Peace! Step lightly on the pebbly shore;
> Calm is the Sea of Love.

ADIEU.

www.ingramcontent.com/pod-product-compliance
Lightning Source LLC
Chambersburg PA
CBHW032143230426
43672CB00011B/2436